Lyming

A PICTORIAL PAST

Lymington

A PICTORIAL PAST

Including Pennington, Boldre and Sway

BRIAN J. DOWN

First published in 1991 by Ensign Publications
2 Redcar Street
Southampton
Hampshire
SO1 5LL

ISBN 1 85455 074 8

Publisher : David Graves
Typesetting : PageMerger
Cover Design : Mark Smith
Second Edition printed in Singapore under the supervision of
MRM Graphics, Winslow, Bucks.

Contents

Contents

Introduction

Lymington's pre-history began with its importance as a trading port for the Celts of the Iron Age, through its situation close to the lowest point at which its river could be forded. These Ancient Britons built an early Iron Age fort at Ampress, and later, possibly after 500 B.C., another Iron Age fort of some seven acres was constructed at Buckland Rings. This comprised three ramparts and two ditches, which formed a stout defence. These entrenchments, of a large circumference, were captured by Vespasian, second-in-command for the Claudian invasion, in 43 A.D., and survive in a fine state of preservation. Proof of the Romans' occupation of this area came in 1744, when 200 pounds weight of Roman coins were unearthed nearby.

The wide Lymington River was navigable as far as these ports, because it was kept free of silt by the scouring action of the double tides. The settlement was a Juto-Saxon village for around 500 years until the arrival of the Normans – and in the Domesday Book of 1086 it is named Lentune, when six villagers worked for Fulkwin, sub-tenant to the Earl of Shrewsbury. Soon after the Conquest it was a Manor given by William I to this Norman lord. The Manor went on to become the property of the influential de Redvers family and their descendants the Courtenays; these families were the overlords of Lymington for almost 500 years.

Lymington has no Charter from the Crown. Earl William de Redvers was quick to note the opportunity to profit from a market and fair – and his Charter of privileges, granted between 1184 and 1216, formed the Borough of New Lymington, added to by Earl Baldwin around 1256. So Lymington is one of the towns in England to receive a Charter from a feudal lord with no intervention from the Crown.

The burgesses elected their own reeve, later known as mayor. The first known mayor was Adam Carpenter, appointed in 1412. In 1685 the then mayor of the town, Thomas Dore, raised a local troop of horse to join the Duke of Monmouth – they failed to reach him in time for the Battle of Sedge-moor, where the Duke was defeated and the conspirators fled for their lives. Dore returned to Lymington, and was later granted a free pardon.

The earliest Lymington town hall was in a state of disrepair by 1300, and another was constructed in 1463 at Nos. 30 and 31, High Street. The next town hall was built in 1684 on the opposite side of the street by Nos. 93 and 94. This was succeeded by the 1720 structure in the centre of the High Street roadway, with a large meeting room above, and in 1789 George III visited Lymington to receive the mayor and Corporation in this town hall. It was demolished in 1858, thus allowing much freer passage of horse drawn traffic in the High Street. The fifth town hall was constructed in 1913 on the northern side of the town hill, as a result of a bequest by Mrs. Martha Earley that her two houses at 117 and 118, High Street, be given to the Corporation for use as municipal offices. When it was decided these houses were unsuitable for conversion to such a purpose, Mrs. Earley's sister, Mrs. Ellen Hewitt, generously defrayed the cost of a new town hall on the site, and she duly laid the foundation stone on February 12th, 1913. These premises served as the Council offices until a more modern building was erected off Avenue Road, which Her Majesty the Queen graciously opened in July, 1966.

Lymington returned two Members of Parliament from the days of Elizabeth I, its first representatives being Anthony Cooke and Richard Cooke, elected in 1584. Amongst the town's other Parliamentarians have been mayor Thomas Dore (1689) following his pardon; Sir Joseph Jekyll (1713), Master of the Rolls; and Edward Gibbon (1781), the historian. The passing of the Representation of the People Act, 1867, resulted in the Borough returning just one M.P., and by the Redistribution of Seats Act, 1885, was merged with the New Forest division. Lymington's last Member of Parliament was the Hon. John Scott Montagu. For a short while Lymington later became a joint constituency with Christchurch, when Robert Adley was elected.

Some of Lymington's 17th and 18th Century

buildings remain 5½-yards wide – the old rod, pole or perch measure – showing it was a planned borough. Its roads remained in an appalling state until the Turnpike Act of 1765. Repairs had been carried out by six days a year of statute labour, ploughing the surface before laying faggots in the deepest ruts: in 1685 it was stated that £2 10s. 4d. was spent on road maintenance. When turnpike gates were set up at entrances to the town, the tolls collected enabled a much higher standard of highway to be introduced on those roads. The only means of illuminating the streets at night was by way of oil lamps placed outside large residences. Gas street lamps were introduced in 1832, and later Lymington had the distinction of becoming one of the first towns along the South Coast to convert to electric street lamps. However, the mayor and several councillors were shareholders in the Lymington Gas & Coke Company, so the street lights reverted back to gas.

In 1345, during the reign of Edward III, Lymington furnished nine ships and 159 men for the French invasion, almost double the number provided by Portsmouth. Lymington had become a port of considerable significance, particularly as the town was a principal manufacturer of fine quality salt for more than 700 years. An uninterrupted line of 163 salt pans stretched along the coastline between Lymington River and Hurst Castle. Windmills, some 12-feet high, pumped the sea water into tanks on stilts, and thence by gravity into the various pans, until they reached the condition of brine, before being lifted into large brick sheds used as boiling houses. These sheds were filled with steam when working, and surrounding roads became blackened with coal-ash from the incessantly burning furnaces. Each pan produced around three tons of salt per week, burning 19 bushels of coal for each ton – so that at one time Lymington imported more coal than London. However, both the salt and the coal for the boiling houses were heavily taxed till 1825. By the end of the 18th Century most of the salt works were in the hands of the local bankers, Messrs. St. Barbe. After the salt trade died, through the excessive taxation and cheaper Cheshire mined salt being transported on improved roads and the new railways, the Lymington marshes were levelled for grazing. They became a principal provider for many families living in the Woodside and Pennington areas, who hunted wildfowl, rabbits, fish and shellfish for their regular sustenance.

From very early times petty dues were levied by the inhabitants on various items of merchandise brought into the port of Lymington. But this right was challenged by the superior Port of Southampton, which led to a court case in 1328, when the verdict went against Lymington. Nevertheless in 1730, having again taken these dues, Lymingtonians were once more sued by the Corporation of Southampton – but on this occasion the clause was removed as judgment was given in Lymington's favour at the County Assize Court.

From the time of the French Revolution until the conclusion of the Napoleonic Wars, 1792 to 1815, large numbers of French immigrants landed at Lymington, leading to several of their regiments being stationed in the town. The 600 men of the Royal French Marine, commanded by Count d'Hector, were barracked in the old Manor House and surrounding farmland at Buckland. The French Artillery, under their commander Colonel Rochalier, were housed in the Malthouse and nearby buildings in New Lane. French refugee soldiers in the Corps of Loyal Emigrants used Quadrille Court in St. Thomas' Street as their quarters. Many later perished in the La Vendee expedition.

The Dowager Lady Blakiston died at Lymington in 1862 at the great age of 102 – she was the widow of Sir Matthew Blakiston, whose father was Lord Mayor of London in 1760, and in such official capacity attended the Coronation of George III. William Ingham Whitaker, of Pylewell Park, died on September 26th, 1893, leaving a fortune of almost £1-million, of which he bequeathed £50,000 to charities.

Another native of Lymington was John Tutchin, whose severe sentence pronounced by the notorious Judge Jeffreys at Dorchester in 1685 brought tears into the eyes of those attending the court. Tried for seditious words, young Tutchin was, as usual, interrupted in his defence by ribaldry and scurrility from the judgment seat: "You are a rebel, and all your family have been rebels since Adam. They tell me that you are a poet. I'll cap verse for you," taunted the Judge. He pronounced sentence that Tutchin should be imprisoned for seven years, and during that period he be flogged through every market town in Dorset each year. The women in the court galleries burst into tears. The clerk of the arraigns stood up in great disorder, and boldly stated: "My Lord, the prisoner is very young. There are many market towns in our county. The sentence amounts to whipping once a fortnight for seven years." The Judge remained unrepentant, replying: "If he is a young man, he is an old rogue. Ladies, you do not know the villain as well as I do. The punishment is not half bad enough for him. All the interest in England shall not alter it." Tutchin despairingly petitioned that he might be hanged instead. Fortunately for him, he was taken ill with smallpox – and as it seemed the sentence would never be carried out, the Chief Justice agreed to remit it in return for a bribe which reduced the prisoner to poverty, and the entire experience left him in a state of madness.

From about 1900, two annual events were eagerly anticipated by Lymington inhabitants – the Flower Show, and the Regatta. The Flower Show brought thousands to its grounds for happy animation and hearty enjoyment. During the evening the grounds were illuminated by coloured electric lights, for open-air dancing to the accompaniment of the Lymington Town Band. The annual Regatta was exceedingly popular, and the daytime amusements brought thousands of people thronging to the riverbanks to witness the sailing and rowing. The scene shifted to the High Street in the evening, brilliantly lit by thousands of small electric fairy lights. Confetti showered down, the Town Band played on a platform, stump speeches were offered, and groups of entertainers sang well into the night.

In 1932 the Borough of Lymington was considerably extended to take in New Milton, Milford, Hordle and Pennington, whose inhabitants raised a considerable outcry at the loss of their own Councils. The next local government change came in 1974, when the Borough was abolished and swallowed up into the New Forest District Council, with its headquarters at Lyndhurst. The Charter Trustees were set up to oversee the old Borough's affairs, but had no real powers. Consequently, as a result of agitation by Lymington Community Association, the District Council agreed to create four Neighbourhood Councils to be elected in Lymington, New Milton, Milford and Hordle – and in 1979 Lymington and New Milton were both granted Town Council status, whilst Hordle and Milford became Parish Councils – and all were afforded the right to add their individual precepts on to the rates.

Boldre

Boldre appears in the Domesday Book as Bovre. Whilst excavating 12-feet below the surface of a gravel pit at Bull Hill in December, 1926, Mr. Gregory unearthed four flint implements, which the British Museum ranked amongst the finest to be discovered and may date back to 25,000 B.C. Boldre was at one time a large and important parish centred on its Norman church, and itself a sub-minster of Christchurch Priory. Both Lymington and Brockenhurst churches are described in early records as Chapels, subservient to Boldre Church. The original organ was given to the church in 1855 by Mrs. Shrubb, widow of the Vicar, the Rev. Charles Shrubb, and was reconstructed from parts of the huge organ which was shown at the Great Exhibition of 1851 held at Crystal Palace, London: modern improvements, including an electric blower to replace the manually operated bellows, were added during a second reconstruction in 1890 at a cost of £150. This organ was removed by a Dutch organ builder in 1989 and replaced by an electronic instrument. In much earlier days, a barrel-organ was situated in a gallery over the western door of the church which played three tunes: the "Old Hundredth", another hymn, and a psalm, which was also accompanied by a flute player.

Boldre's parish registers of baptisms, marriages and burials date from 1596, and include such unusual surnames as Headach, America, Strawbery, Longears, Sweetapple, Livelong, Needle and Farthing. As was commonplace along the local shoreline, smuggling was a productive occupation at Boldre. At Pitts Deep, kegs of spirits were roped together before being sunk about a quarter-mile offshore, at a spot known as Brandy Hole, and marked by a float. Later, at an opportune moment, the kegs were floated ashore by punts – so that it was easier to sink them if a coastguard should suddenly arrive on the scene unannounced – then they were furtively carried by local men to waiting horses and carts.

In 1784 Monsieur Blanchard, the French balloonist, made his ascent from a barracks in London and was carried southwards by the wind. His balloon was spotted by the owners and servants of Pylewell House as Monsieur Blanchard floated over the Solent, before the winds changed direction and forced him to land at Romsey. When the famous artist Thomas Rowlandson visited the Lymington area in 1786, he illustrated Pylewell House and this earliest balloon flight in Hampshire.

In the year 1836 the Vicar, Charles Shrubb, rented the fishing in the Boldre River for £11 – and between July 9th and October 14th he landed 13 salmon, one trout, 32 mullet, 105 bass, one eel and 24 flatfish. The following year Mr. Shrubb rented Mr. Morant's stream above Boldre Bridge from June 29th till September 11th for £15, and his recorded catch during that period included 127 salmon.

The subservient links of the Lymington curacy with Boldre church ended in 1869, when the Reverend Benjamin Maturin was accorded the status of Vicar of Lymington.

Pennington

The Manor of Pennington was held in thirds by three different owners from the time of Henry of Thistledon in 1285, until John Pulteney made it one Manor in 1834. A chapel, named Magdalen Chapel, once stood in Pennington, its earliest mention being in 1276. It was used for worship until the reign of Elizabeth I. Until 1839 Pennington was ecclesiastically and civilly part of Milford, before it became a separate parish. On March 13th, 1839, its church was consecrated by the Bishop of Winchester under the patronage of St. Mark. A barrel-organ in the church played two tunes: the "Old Hundredth" and the National Anthem.

Of high Victorian architectural merit was Pennington School in the village square, opened in September, 1852. A clock was added to its bell-turret by public subscription to mark the Coronation of King George V. The need for extra accommodation with a rising number of pupils led to an infants' school being erected close by in 1886-87. Pennington womenfolk often placed their laundry to dry on the gorse bushes on Pennington Common. The village was dubbed "Donkey Town" on account of the great number of these animals which their owners grazed on the Common. New council housing developments following the Second World War led to a great influx of new inhabitants into Pennington.

1 · The Importance of Salt

Lymington was once a busy port, and during the time of Edward I was a considerable place of entry for French wines and other commodities. It has been said that Lymington supplied more ships than Southampton at the time of the Armada – and certainly during the reign of Edward III Lymington furnished nine ships and 159 men for the defence of the realm, almost double that of Portsmouth. The river was once navigable as far as Ampress and its forts, and was considerably wider and deeper. In the time of the de Redvers, the Earls, as Lords of the Manor, claimed the whole of the estuary and exacted tolls and dues, and when they gave the Charter to the Burgesses, such rights passed on to them. Around 1720, Daniel Defoe complained of "rogueing and smuggling" as being a major industry around Lymington and Pennington. Several of the town's 45 inns were used as headquarters by smugglers, and underground passages were dug to hide such contraband as brandy and fine silks before they were spirited away.

For more than 700 years Lymington was a principal manufacturer of salt. By 1660 as much coal for the salterns was handled at Lymington as in London, with ships of up to 1,300 tons berthing at the Quay to load and unload. Along the coastline between Lymington and Hurst there was an unbroken line of 163 salt pans, which brought great wealth to the town. These salterns comprised shallow pans around 25 feet square, with mudbanks six inches high, where the salt evaporated. Sixteen weeks' boiling was the general season average, each pan providing about three tons of salt weekly, with 19 bushels of coal burned for each ton.

At their most prosperous time, 1750, no less than £60,000 was paid in one year as duty, and by 1804 the amount of fine salt manufactured reached 6,000 tons per annum. More than half was exported to such distant places as America, Newfoundland, Holland and the Baltic, on board such ships as the *Charming Sally*, the *Dolphin*, and *Sea Horse* which left Lymington Quay for the three-months' Atlantic round trip. But in 1808 there was a great local outcry when the Government duty had reached 15 shillings a bushel, whereas the actual value of the salt was merely one shilling. The trade had ceased by 1845, when cheaper salt from the Cheshire mines could be readily transported by rail.

2 · Captain Cross and his Illegal Toll Bridge

Charles I, looking to raise money or to pay debts without money passing, granted to Robert Pamplin, "in consideration of a great debt and faithful service done", all the mud-lands between Calshot and Hurst Castle. In 1731, a Merchant Captain, William Cross of Boldre, a descendant of Pamplin, took it upon himself to build a dam across Lymington River. This action greatly upset the Corporation, so the mayor Charles Powlett made a written protest: "Whereas Captain Cross hath lately erected across the River a Bank or Dam, whereby it is apprehended the navigation will be greatly injured (if not in time totally destroyed) unless some method be taken to prevent it. It is therefore ordered that the Town Clarke do state a proper case, and lay the same before Counsell, and report his opinion to the Mayor and Burgesses, when assembled at the Town Hall; and that the Town Clarke doe bring an Action of Trespass against the said Captain Cross at the suite of the Mayor and Burgesses, for digging and carrying away the land at Bridge Green, which was then in the possession of the Corporation." Mr. Charles Colbourne acted as Counsel.

Captain Cross died prior to the action coming before Winchester Assizes in 1739, which went against the Corporation – so that, to the chagrin of Lymington townsfolk, the Captain's widow and a tailor William Lyne duly exacted a toll on all who passed over the dam or bridge. Ship owners were similarly annoyed, as the toll bridge effectively prevented the scouring action of the tides, causing the river to silt up. In 1899 King Edward VII was enjoying one of his first ever car rides, as a passenger of the second Lord Montagu; having passed through the Forest, they were made to wait for an inordinately long time at the toll bridge for, to the distinct amusement of the King, gatekeeper Mr. G. Gooden was vexed after an earlier driver had sped over the bridge without paying. Tolls continued to be exacted until 1958.

This 1907 photograph shows a lady pedestrian paying her dues at the toll-keeper's office. The inn is the *Freemasons' Arms*, and the large signboard advertises: "Milk per glass 2d., Bovril per cup 4d., Biscuits and cheese 2d., Biscuits 1d., Lime juice 2d., Ginger beer 2d., Cyder per glass 2d. Cigars and cigarettes. Spirits, ales, etc., at moderate prices."

Tollgate, Lymington.

3 · The Lymington–Yarmouth Paddle Steamers

Crossing from Lymington to the Isle of Wight could often be hazardous, with the strong Solent tides and winds, until in 1830 the arrival of the paddle-steamer *Glasgow* made for much more comfortable passage. Built of wood two years earlier at Newcastle, the 54′ steamer went into regular service on April 5th, 1830, leaving from the railway station harbour near the Quay. Passengers had to share the boat with horse drawn carriages and cattle until tow-boat barges (see also chapter 74) were introduced in 1836, towing goods and live-stock from the stern. In 1841 the 82′ Southampton-built *Solent* was also introduced, sailing three times a week from Lymington to Yarmouth, Cowes, Ryde and Portsmouth. Timetables showed that on Sundays, the crossings to Yarmouth departed at "9 a.m. and 2½ p.m." The ferry enterprise was carried out by Lymington businessmen until the Solent Steam Packet was formed in 1842.

The *Glasgow* was withdrawn in 1852, and six years later the 54-ton *Red Lion* came on service, built at North Shields, and making four daily cross-ings to Yarmouth. In 1861 the first *Solent* was decommissioned, to be replaced two years later by the new 94′ *Solent*, (pictured left), which had been constructed at Lymington. In 1866 the fleet was increased to three paddle-steamers with the arrival of 98′ *Mayflower* (pictured on the right) from New-castle, and some 14 years later the *Red Lion* was withdrawn.

When the Steam Packet company was bought out by the London & S.W. Railway in 1879, they purchased the *Solent* and *Mayflower* for £2,750. In 1882 the railway track was extended out to Lymington Pier, as the passenger boat service had previously been restricted by tidal conditions around the Quay. With crossings increased to six each day, in 1893 the much larger *Lymington* was added to the fleet, 120′ long and constructed of steel at Southampton, the saloon being upholstered in velvet. Another Southampton built boat, the third *Solent* entered service in 1902, with a 101′ long promenade deck comprising a first-class saloon aft, and enclosed passenger shelter forward. Later, the bridge was enclosed in a teak wheelhouse, and she continued on service from Lymington until 1948.

4 · Local Outcry Over New Water Supply

Lymington's water was supplied by wells, of which there were over 600 in the district, but a third of these were contaminated by drainage from unventilated brick sewers and dirty water from laundries. There was a brick sewer in the High Street, but none in St. Thomas' Street; a sewer in Church Lane once ran open in the street – whilst the South Street (Captain's Row), Gosport Street and Station Street sewer discharged direct into the Quay, to the considerable annoyance of residents there.

On January 15th, 1867, representation was made to the Local Board, calling for sanitary improvements owing to the deteriorating state of the water and drainage arrangements. Dr. Airey, the first medical officer appointed, reminded the Board of their shortcomings in his annual reports. But many residents were opposed to such innovative ideas, preferring a system of middens (dunghills) and ashpits. The Town Clerk wrote to "The Times" quoting medical opinion to this effect, as two–thirds of the townsfolk, aghast at such extravagant expenditure, insisted they would refuse to be connected to any water supply or sewerage system.

Such was the outcry that a Residents' Association was formed, and members' feelings were reflected by a letter, signed "An old Inhabitant", which was published in "The Lymington Chronicle" on August 17th, 1883: "People who don't like smells must hold their noses … if health suffers, send for a doctor, and take physic. If all nuisances were abolished, there would be no doctors and people would live too long. It is absurd to be too particular in these matters. Local Boards are no good."

Various schemes were proposed during this verbal conflict. A new well was sunk at great expense near Apsley House, but was abandoned as sand was often found in the water. Another well was sunk at Southampton Buildings for £1,400, but the cylindrical walls collapsed and sand infiltrated. Finally, engineers Easton & Anderson bored a site at Ampress, a water tower was erected next to the Sports Ground in 1883, and the following year the scheme was completed for £8,500. Connections were gradual, as many preferred their own wells. In 1908 an artesian well was sunk at Ampress, and after three months of boring the water burst through at a great height. One councillor witnessing this great occasion was so overcome that he immediately knelt to offer a prayer of thanksgiving. A second artesian bore was sunk, the total sum borrowed for the water supply being £14,173 3s. 2d. The Council built this second water tower pictured below, near Buckland Rings, in 1932.

5 · Life on Lymington Quay

Seen in the foreground is one of the halfpenny rowing ferries which regularly crossed from the Quay to a pontoon on the opposite side of the river. The oarsman is Billy Cruse (see also p.22). On the main Quay, huge tree trunks were frequently offloaded from ships for local timber merchants – children from the neighbourhood loved playing hide and seek amongst these trunks. Shingle was also brought in on boats for the building trade.

Beyond this was the coalyard quay, where two-masted ships carrying up to 100 tons of coal would tie up. The coal would be weighed up into one-hundredweight sacks on board the boat, with one man shovelling and another on a winch hauling up the coal. Men would then run up and down "the monkey" gangplanks to bring the coal ashore on to the wharf. The whole operation involved up to twelve men.

Young boys living around the Quay would dive into the river to retrieve lumps of coal which had spilled from the boats on to the riverbed. It was not unknown for whole hundredweight sacks to "inadvertently" fall into the river during the offloading operations. Beyond this coal wharf was another quay, where imported bricks were brought in by ship.

Behind these wharves, along Quay Street, was the Bethel House, which acted as a mission for sailors who attended religious services there.

A great many parents in Lymington forbade their young children to venture anywhere near the Quay, owing to its reputation for uncivil behaviour amongst some of the residents living there, aggravated by the number of ale houses packed into such a confined area. Despite such infamy, these families around the Quay always rallied in support if their neighbours fell upon ill times. Canon Lane was of similar repute.

6 · The Making-Up of Avenue Road

This photograph, taken before the turn of the century, shows the first construction of Avenue Road, between Buckland and Southampton Road, through Barfields. Local folk had grown corn and vegetable crops in these fields, which were left open every autumn in order that horses and cattle could graze on the land.

Imported chalk was used to form the foundations of Avenue Road. This was placed into wheelbarrows, which the workmen pushed up the wooden gangplanks held high with trestles at one end, whilst wooden barrels were used for stability at the other end, as shown in this picture. The men would then tip the chalk into tip-up trucks waiting beneath the planks. Horses would haul these trucks along a railway track in the middle of the road, and the chalk emptied at required points along the highway. The first vehicle to pass along the completed, gravelled Avenue Road was a horse-drawn hearse, carrying the body of a typhoid patient who had died in the Fever Hospital, next to the Poorhouse (Infirmary). The coffin was borne out to Lymington Cemetery, along Cemetery Road, since renamed Highfield Avenue.

At the far end of the road can be seen the ivy covered *Borough Arms*, which dates back to 1855 as a posting house, and three years later it became the *Clipper Arms* (a Clipper was a light chaise hauled by two horses). The Jolliffe family held the licence of this establishment for many years after 1859, and their early billheads bore the proud boast: "The oldest established Post Masters in Lymington". With the telephone number Lymington 9, J. Jolliffe & Son offered many forms of transport in 1910: "Large and small Brakes to carry 22, 16, 12 or 10 persons. Invalid pony chairs. Landaus, Broughams, Victorias, Dog Carts, Pony and other Carriages. Post horses. Drivers who know the Forest well. Washington Cars and Mourning Coaches at the shortest notice and at moderate charges."

7 · The Parish Church of St. Thomas

Parts of St. Thomas' Church date back to around 1250, though the town had a chapel long before that time, possibly on the same site. The church is dedicated to St. Thomas the Apostle, and about 1325 a mortuary chapel was added. The first known incumbent was William Ekerdon, in 1396. At the Reformation, the church was annexed to the Priory Church of Christchurch, who appointed a curate or chaplain, and an £8 annual rent was imposed under a 1504 lease. On the Dissolution of Monasteries, the Crown seized the Rectory of Lymington as part of the possessions of Christchurch, but two years later, in 1542, under Henry VIII, the Lymington Rectory was granted to the Bishop of Bristol as part of his endowment. He took the emoluments of the Vicarage, but with no resident clergyman, "things spiritual" in Lymington began to suffer.

For many years there was only one monthly service, and the burial of the dead was performed by the parish clerk. In 1586 the Rev. Robert Jackson, Vicar of Boldre, claimed the Lymington tithes, but this was successfully resisted by parishioners. The church was gutted when occupied by Puritan soldiers during the civil wars, but the inhabitants of the town later repaired the damage, and in 1670 the south transept was pulled down and the present church tower erected. A peal of bells was installed in 1671, when £26 12s. was paid to the bell-founders at Romsey; a clock was added to the tower in 1674. Until 1831, the hymn singing was accompanied by a small orchestra, but that year a fine organ, built by Mr. Walker of London for £475, was erected from public subscription. Mr. Philip Klitz was the first organist, and Henry Frances Lyte, author of the hymn "Abide with Me", once held the curacy at Lymington.

In 1869, at the Court of Balmoral, Queen Victoria signed an Order separating the Chapelry of Lymington from the Vicarage of Boldre, decreeing that the benefice should be vested in the Bishop of Winchester. Queen Victoria did, in fact, pay a fleeting visit to St. Thomas' Church, whilst crossing the Solent in the royal yacht during a sojourn at Osborne House on the Isle of Wight. The eastern and western clock faces were illuminated in memory of the Rev. Benjamin Maturin, Vicar of Lymington from 1852 until his death in 1905. The Parish Hall was built for church use at the western end of Emsworth Road in 1928.

Valentine   *High Street, Lymington*

8 · A Bridge to Link Lymington and Walhampton

In March, 1834, Mr. Richard Andrew Grove published these plans for a proposed suspension bridge across the Lymington River, thereby freeing residents from the impositions of either the halfpenny rowing-boat ferries which crossed from the Quay, or of having to use the toll bridge which had been built without permission in 1731. Designed by architect Mr. Benjamin Ferrey, the suspension bridge would have formed a continuation of Quay Hill to create a link with Walhampton.

Mr. Grove pronounced that the suspension bridge was designed "to remove all obstructions to an uninterrupted intercourse between the Town and a highly respectable portion of the Neighbourhood and thereby relieve the Inhabitants of Tax exceeding £1,000 a year, and will, it is hoped, prove a sufficient recommendation to the Public to induce their ready support of a plan for erecting a Free Bridge in the eligible situation pointed out in the above Sketch".

The suspension bridge, he explained, would extend for 300 feet over the centre of the River, comprising a solid Causeway of 130 feet, faced with stone and surmounted with a parapet, to form an abutment to each end of the Bridge. The Bridge and Causeway was to be 26 feet wide, including two pathways, with the roadway of the Bridge seven feet above high water. The whole new line of road, including the Bridge, from the top of Quay Hill to the road upon the east side of Mr. Good's marsh, was 1,350 feet. The total estimate of the Bridge and Causeway to the design was £6,000; estimate of the property to be purchased for forming the approaches to the Bridge, a further £3,000.

In proclaiming his plan, Mr. Grove told the public: "It is admitted by persons conversant with the subject, that the Suspension is a very economical, ornamental, safe, and durable mode of erecting bridges. A stone bridge of the extent requisite for a free admission of the tide, as represented in the above design, could not be completed for double the cost of one upon the above principle. The quiet situation of the harbour and the firm gravelly state of the bed of the river are much in favour of the safety of any

bridge that may be constructed; and the line this Bridge would take over the river would not obstruct the usual navigation. A considerable portion of the mud which has accumulated in the harbour, much to the inconvenience of the navigation, might be removed and mixed with shingle to fill up the space between the walls of the causeway; and it is too evident that if something be not speedily done in this way to cleanse the bed of the river, it will not, a few years hence, be navigable for vessels exceeding 100 tons."

Mr. Grove contended that he would oppose any suggestions that tolls be imposed upon carriages and horses (allowing foot passengers to pass free) so that some return would be made upon the capital invested, for "I must beg leave to observe that such tolls would barely pay the expense of collection. In towns not half the importance of Lymington capital has been raised of much larger amount than the sum now requisite for the erection of a Suspension Bridge. Indeed it becomes the duty of the inhabitants of all towns, especially upon the coast, where the localities are so inviting to strangers to take up their residence, to promote every reasonable step towards improvement, in order that the public, visiting watering places, should not be induced to congregate in the large and populous towns only."

Mr. Grove stated that many inhabitants had promised unsolicited donations, amounting to very nearly £2,000, towards the proposed bridge, "and I have had the honour of an interview with the noble owner of Beaulieu Manor, who has promised in the most handsome manner to give it his support." Mr. Grove contended that new villas and cottages should be built to let at a rental of £25 to £50 per annum, which would soon be occupied by respectable families, thereby greatly assisting trade and relieving parochial expense. Alas, the suspension bridge never materialised, probably owing to legal and financial difficulties.

Designed by B. Ferrey Architect.

Lith.d by J. Hughe.

PROPOSED SUSPENSION BRIDGE ACROSS THE LYMINGTON RIVER.

Published by R.A. Grove, Lymington, Hants.

9 · The Arrival of Electricity

Lymington residents relied on oil lamps for lighting, and later gas from the Lymington Gas & Coke Company's gasometers in Gosport Street, until the arrival of electricity. In June, 1898, the Lymington Light & Power Co. Ltd. was formed, with the purpose of applying to the Board of Trade for a Provisional Order authorising them to supply electricity in the Borough of Lymington. Sanction for such an Order was confirmed by Parliament the following August. Mr. G.R. Masters, from Jackman & Masters, the estate agents in the High Street, was made secretary of the Electric Light Co., carrying out his duties from an office at 107, High Street.

A February, 1900, edition of "The Lymington Chronicle" newspaper published a preliminary notice announcing "Light is expected to be available next autumn. The Company will, if desired, fit up your house free of all initial expense, only charging the small rental of 1/- per lamp per annum. Schedule of charges for the current: for the first hour per day, 7d per unit; for any further quantity, 4d per unit. Equal to gas at 4/1d and 2/4d per cubic feet. A necessity of modern life." Every household in the Borough received a circular asking for applications for light, to plan the routes for mains and services.

Contract for the entire equipment for the generating station in Bath Road was placed with the Edmundson Electric Corporation Ltd., of Westminster, who took half their payment in shares in the Lymington company, giving them a controlling interest. The generating station was coal-fired, with coal brought from Derbyshire by train, then by horse and cart from Lymington railway station, with each load weighed on the company's own weighbridge. Two 75kw Bellis & Morcom generating sets were coupled to Babcock & Wilcox boilers. In 1931 the supply was changed from DC to AC, and English Electric alternators driven by Mirrlees diesels were installed with a 560kw capacity.

There were strong complaints from Bath Road residents when excessive vibration from these engines caused ornaments and valuables to fall from mantelpieces and shelves. Experts were summoned, and an eventual cure was effected by starting all three diesels simultaneously, then bringing them on load separately so that they were out of synchronisation. The supply was extended to Sway and East End, before the Wessex Electricity Co. took over in 1935. The generating station in Bath Road operated for thirty years before it was closed down.

This 1952 photograph shows the station manager, Mr. Peter Rook snr., lubricating the Mirrlees diesel engines whilst they were driving the generators.

10 · The Unreliable Steam Bus

This Clarkson steam omnibus, registration number LC 1435, began service in the town in 1905, regularly journeying between Lymington and New Milton railway stations, taking in local hotels and occasionally calling at Milford. The vehicle was garaged in a corrugated-iron shed in the Lymington railway station yard. Nevertheless this service proved somewhat unreliable, for the vehicle's 4½-ton weight took its toll on the dirt highways, often sinking into potholes and muddy surfaces, thereby presenting a formidable task to extract. Consequently the 'bus was withdrawn from local service after only 14 months, when it was transferred to Exeter.

The elegant three-storey residence with porch in the photograph is Stanwell House, 15, High Street, originally a gentleman's residence. In 1759 General James Wolfe spent his last night there prior to his departure from Lymington Quay in a longboat, which transported him to his frigate moored in the Solent. From there his British Forces went on to capture Quebec from the French, and by 1763 the whole of the Canadian territory became a British Possession. The owner of Stanwell House was the General's cousin, James Butcher, who died in 1792 and is buried in Lymington churchyard.

The shop at 16, High Street, belonged to Elgar & Son, builders and painters, who had the distinction of being the oldest surviving family business in the town until Peter Elgar retired in 1985. It was his great-grandfather, Benjamin Elgar, who founded the concern in the late 1700s, using a workshop on the riverfront, close to the junction with the toll-bridge road. An 1801 receipt described his work carried out at Lymington Poor House, when laying a closet floor cost 9d., and three-quarters of a day's work making a door frame 2s.1½d. He also became an undertaker, and took over the High Street shop around 1830. The firm had expanded across the Solent to Yarmouth by 1859, when the charge for paper-hanging was ½d. per yard. Elgar's employed fifty men when they built the town hall on the opposite side of the High Street hill in 1913; Quarr House at Sway was another imposing residence constructed by the firm. Elgar's workmen were responsible for the upkeep of the vast private mansions at Pylewell, Walhampton, and Newlands Manor, and luxury yachts from the river were painted. Successive Elgar generations perpetuated the line: grandfather Samuel, father Sidney, and finally Peter. The firm gave up building work in 1960 to concentrate on retail decorating, until 25 years later the business closed and the premises became a 'remainder' bookshop.

11 · The Halfpenny Ferry to Cross the River

In the foreground of this 1905 picture is the wooden pontoon built by Mr. George Turrell, a shipwright at Lymington Shipyard, for the halfpenny rowing ferries which operated from the town Quay. These ferry-boats were owned by Mr. E.R. Badcock, who ran the drapery shop at 41 and 42 High Street, and the estate agents at 91 and 92 on the opposite side of the street, along with an undertaker's business. If mourners requested his personal presence at a funeral, to walk in front of the horse-drawn hearse in his silk hat, he would charge an extra £10 on the bill. He was also a stern magistrate, and when two local men were caught shooting on the marshes on a Sunday, he imposed a severe fine and confiscated their guns.

Mr. Badcock employed several men to row the ferries from one side of the river to the other for a halfpenny, or out to Ferry Point House by the pier for one penny. These ferrymen included Mr. Greenfield, who lived in the shop on the corner of the Quay alongside the river which sold sweets and groceries; "Buzzy" Shutler, who lived in No. 1 cottage at the foot of Union (later East) Hill; Jim Arnold, who had one leg and was accommodated in the lodging house off the Quay; Ruce Miller from Quay Street; his brother Sally Miller from Bath Road; Olly Winkworth, who lived in South Street (later renamed Captain's Row); Billy Cruse, a stoker invalided out of the Royal Navy in the 1920s with infantile paralysis, but despite being a cripple lived in Quay Street until the age of 72; Tom Warren, who lived off the cutting by the lodging house before he died in Knowle Hospital of a mental illness; and Ted "Puffer" Tompkins who, rather the worse for drink whilst rowing a lady passenger out to the pier late one night around 1930, fell out of the boat on his return, clung on to the stern, but after being rescued died of hypothermia despite the administrations of Dr. Pitt.

From 1918 to 1921 Miss Winifred Hopkinson, whose father Charles was manager of the Lymington Gas & Coke Co. in Gosport Street, was employed by Mr. Badcock, and late each afternoon she cycled down to the Quay to collect the halfpennies off the ferrymen. She also had to collect rents from dozens of small houses around the town, cycled as far as Beaulieu to carry out household inventories, when big country mansions were let furnished for a few months at a time, and took bids at auction sales – all for 30/- a week. She later emigrated to South Africa.

12 · The Great Flood of 1909

The low-lying areas around Bath Road and Waterloo Road were always vulnerable to flooding as the river often overflowed during storms. This picture was taken in October, 1909, showing flooding in Waterloo Road near its junction with Bridge Road. It appeared on a post-card of that day, depicting a waterborne relief party ferrying supplies to the house occupants, seen in the bedroom windows of their marooned properties. All manner of items could be seen floating around the riverside areas, with chicken coops from the Lymington side washed up at Walhampton.

On the reverse side of this postcard Mrs. Polly Knight, of 44, Middle Road, Lymington, wrote about the flooding in a message to her husband Will Knight, who was working on the construction of Copythorne Church at the time. He was employed as a plumber by Elgar's in the High Street, and he was also secretary for the New Forest branch of the Painters' & Plumbers' Union.

Polly's communication to her husband ran: "This was October 27th, 1909. Nothing but rain. This is Waterloo Road on Wednesday morning from the Bridge to the Station. There was no trains till quarter to ten. We went down and had a look at it in the afternoon and it was a site, but some of it has gone down. They were afraid it would come back again last night but it did not." The card was first post-marked at Lymington October 29th, 1909, and again at Cadnam the following day.

13 · The Army's Last Duel

On Wednesday, April 13th, 1814, what is reputed to be the Army's last duel took place on Pennington Common. The combatants were Captain William Souper and Lieutenant John Dieterich. Souper considered he had been insulted by his adversary, who refused to apologise. The pistol duel was arranged to be fought near the bathing houses alongside Lymington River, but as the contest was about to take place a constable appeared there, so the two men rode in a waiting post-chaise to Pennington Common. The constable pursued, but by the time he had reached the Common the duellists were already in position, and their seconds moving back.

Dieterich was first to fire, but missed his intended victim. When the more accurate Captain returned fire, Dieterich collapsed to the ground. As the policeman approached, Souper and his second rode off in the chaise back to Lymington. The constable followed in an abortive pursuit, before returning to Pennington Common, where he encountered the chaise collecting the injured Lieut. Dieterich – who was taken to Lymington, where surgeon Mr. Knight found a wound in the right hip which led to the backbone, from whence he extracted a ball.

Dieterich died two days later, on April 15th, and was buried in Lymington churchyard. There the inscription on his headstone read: "The Service has been deprived of a very meritorious officer, his wife of an excellent husband, and his children of a truly tender father."

The duellists' two seconds gave themselves up, anticipating charges of manslaughter, but after preliminary hearings their cases were not proceeded with. Souper found himself in the dock at Hampshire Assizes in July, 1814, charged with murder, unaware that the Government had recently issued an edict on judges, calling on them to stamp out duelling by inflicting heavy sentences. Several witnesses testified to Souper's good character, but Mr. Justice Dampier's summing-up convinced the defendant he was subject to capital punishment. The jury took 30 minutes to issue a guilty verdict, whereupon Souper collapsed to the floor with a loud groan. He recovered to recall his honourable service for the country, before the Judge pronounced a sentence of death by hanging, on a date set for July 25th. But Mr. Justice Dampier successfully recommended clemency, and Souper in fact soon returned to his Army career, finally retiring in 1835.

Pennington Common.

14 · William Gilpin – the Popular Vicar

Soon after the afforestation of the New Forest by William I in 1079, work began on the construction of the church at Boldre – second only in antiquity within the New Forest to St. Nicholas', Brockenhurst. The only remaining part of the Norman church at Boldre are the three inner-most arches of the south arcade with their piers and the respond at the east end. Early in the 14th century the chancel and lower part of the tower were built; the upper section of the tower was rebuilt in brick at the end of the 17th century. In 1561 Boldre church-goers secured their independence from Christ-church, after determined refusals to pay their arrears of pension.

On the north wall of the chapel is a wall tablet in memory of a previous Vicar, the Rev. William Gilpin, a remarkable man. Gilpin took up the post in 1777, and on his arrival was astounded at the lawless-ness of parishioners: "exposed to every pillage and robbery, from their proximity to the deer, the game, and the fuel of the New Forest, the lower class of parishioners being little better than a gang of gypsies."

Nevertheless the popular Vicar introduced a great deal of reform amongst his flock. His innovations included a school on the corner of Pilley Hill and School Lane for the education of twenty boys and twenty girls, the children of day labourers of the parish. They were segregated into separate class-rooms, where the boys were taught "reading, writing, and the first four rules of arithmetic," and the girls "to read, knit or spin, sew or mend their own clothes". The master's salary amounted to £24 per annum, and the mistress's £12. The school was opened on July 1st, 1791, and cost £400 with equip-ment. Gilpin was determined to endow it, so set to work to produce a great many sketches and draw-ings, often executed by candlelight, which were sold on May 6th, 1802, for £1,200. He also built and organised the Boldre Poor House, admired by social reformers of that day. Gilpin died in 1804, and was buried in the churchyard. His school continued operating until 1875, when it was converted into Gilpin's Cottage and the 118 pupils moved into a larger school on the opposite side of the road. The 200th anniversary celebrations were marked in 1991.

St. John's Church contains the only memorial for H.M.S. *Hood*, the battleship sunk during the Second World War. On May 24th, 1941, she was hit off Iceland by the guns of the prize German battleship *Bismarck* – she sank within two minutes, with the loss of Admiral Holland and 1,416 officers and men – there were only three survivors. The Admiral and his family were regular worshippers at Boldre.

Boldre Church, near Lymington

15 · Oldest Family Business in the South

King's the booksellers and stationers once claimed to be the oldest family business on the South Coast. In 1735 schoolmaster John King had set up a small printing plant in Yeovil, Somerset. When he died in 1762, eldest son John jnr. took over, whilst third son Charles (born 1744) became a bookseller in Dorchester, where he successfully advertised for a wife before moving on to Lymington in 1805. Here he was kept extremely busy attending the business of the 4,000 French royalists barracked here, in addition to the English regiments and local residents.

Charles and his wife Eleanor had no progeny, but in 1817 nephew Richard (born 1796) walked the considerable distance from Yeovil to Lymington to join his uncle in the family business at 126, High Street, when bookbinders and printers toiled daily from 7 a.m. till 8 p.m. Richard married Elizabeth Jones, the girl next door, and they had four children. To counter the opposition of three other printers by now in Lymington, Richard journeyed to London for the first time in his life to purchase a printing press and books at such favourable rates that he was able to undercut his rivals by large margins. Richard died in 1877, after second son Edward (born 1821) had taken over the business, and in 1858 they had moved to the present address of 105, High Street: soon afterwards No. 106 was added. In the early 18th century this had been a chemist's shop – and Edward converted the music room into a printing works. But such was the growing demand for printing work of all kinds, ranging from billheads to the "Registers of the Dutch Church of Austin Friars", edited by Mr. Moens of Boldre which took some 30 years to produce, that a specific print machine shop was erected to the rear of the premises. The old music room was then utilised as a compositors' room until, in 1904, the machine shop was extended to accommodate the compositors. In 1879 Edward wrote the authoritative "Old Times Revisited", which subsequently became a reference book on the history of the town.

The hand presses were duly succeeded by steam machines, and eventually by electric motors. Edward, three times mayor of Lymington, died in 1885 and the business was carried on by second son Charles, with brother Richard as partner until the latter left for London to start his own publishing enterprise in Tabernacle Street. Soon embarking on printing and publishing the standard works of fiction, Richard was reputed to be the first man to publish a cloth bound book for one shilling, which he sold in vast numbers. Nevertheless, an enterprise on such a scale required financial capital, and his desperate reduction of wholesale prices in a bid to sell even greater quantities led to a gradual decline of the business, which was eventually closed down. Meantime Charles married Mrs. Annie Gladding (nee Swinstead) in 1886, and eight years later was elected mayor of Lymington.

The youngest of his four children, Edward (born 1893), continued the business and in 1927, 13 years after his father's death, married Lilian Graham and went on to publish a fine history of Lymington including recollections of his boyhood days in "A Walk Through Lymington" (also published by Ensign Publications). The shop area had been doubled in 1955 by utilising the old hall and dining room, and in 1968 the entire basement and old kitchens were converted into a paperback and children's books department and stock-room. In 1982 the stationery stock and new offices were sited in the old printing works. Many well-known personalities have visited the shop in recent years for book-signing sessions, amongst them round-the-world sailors Alec Rose and Robin Knox-Johnson, Prime Minister Edward Heath, and broadcaster Robert Dougall.

Edward had two daughters, the eldest of whom, Miss Mary King, succeeded as managing director of the business following her father's death in 1974, assisted by sister Janet's husband David Irvine. Mary died in 1987, just months before the long-planned management buy-out by Alan and Dodie Bishop, Nikki Leitch and Gordon Young. This 1877 photograph shows, left to right: Edward King, Charles King with elder brother Richard and their printers Meadows, Loader and Gatrell.

16 · The Lymington River Sailing Club

The Royal Lymington Yacht Club headquarters, photographed after considerable extensions and renovations had been undertaken by local builders G.G. Harvey. The Club's beginnings date back to the early days of 1914, when Captain H.H. Nicholson and 17 other members formed the Lymington River Sailing Club, with the intention of racing Lymington Pram dinghies built for £20 by Dan Bran in his nearby riverside shed. They staged weekly races between May 15th and August 15th – but before they could hold their first annual meeting, the country had gone to war against Germany. So the Club disbanded, and boom defences were placed in the western Solent, with guns installed at Hurst Castle and Fort Victoria.

Peaceful sailing resumed on the river as war ended in 1918, when Lymington Harbour Master Captain Harper paddled his way in a duck punt to collect 5/- annual harbour dues for the Pram dinghies, and rather more for larger craft. A member of the Royal Yacht Squadron, Major Cyril Potter, O.B.E., lived in a house called Blakes which has been renamed Ferry Point. There he invited six men and four ladies to a meeting, where it was unanimously agreed to re-form the Lymington River Sailing Club in 1922; the annual subscription was a guinea, or 10/- for members living outside a ten-mile radius of Lymington Church. Major Potter's cruiser Wendy formed the start-line. In 1923 Lymington Council transferred the lease of the Coastguard boathouse to the newly formed L.R.S.C.; the property, site and slipway cost £600, and a further £1,253 was spent on improvements. Though the clubhouse remained closed during the winter months, fund-raising continued, varying from amateur dramatics to hiring the premises for private parties, until debts were cleared by March, 1929. Harvey's the builders removed the slate roof and raised the walls to create a large clubroom, and walls from the old building still form part of today's southern wing.

In December, 1925, the Admiralty Warrant was granted, and the following April the L.R.S.C. was renamed the Lymington Yacht Club. In 1926 application was made for the Royal Warrant, but King George VI did not sign his approval until November 3rd, 1938. To preserve the high social standing of the membership, those connected with the word "trade" were unhesitatingly excluded. The Club's XOD division is the third oldest of its class, dating back to 1927 with eight boats, their first captain being Admiral Sir Sackville Carden of the Gallipoli tragedy.

17 · History of Lymington's Post Offices

Lymington's first Post Office was operated by Richard Galpins with his bookselling and printing business at 88, High Street, which he occupied from 1806-36. That shop was occupied in 1840 by Robert Klitz, who boasted "The oldest Music Business in the South of England, having been established in 1789". The town's second Post Office was close by at 84, High Street, run by the printer and bookseller Charles Watterson. The next Post Office operated from 71, High Street, later to become Sillis' then Webb's shoe shops. In 1905 the Post Office moved across the road to 55, High Street, where it was to remain until, in 1960, the old Home Mead building next door at No. 54, a one-time mansion which became Mersley School until allowed to remain empty and fall into a state of disrepair during the Second World War, was acquired by compulsory purchase. This continues to be the main Post Office in the town.

Other sub-Post Offices were opened around the town for the convenience of customers. Near the foot of the town hill, No. 127 became the High Street East Post Office, run by Mrs. Sadler and her spinster daughter. Waterford Post Office was managed by Harold Beagley; there were others at Pennington and Buckland – plus the one below photographed around 1920, Highfield Post Office, in the Ava Terrace, Western Road home of Mr. and Mrs. Burridge. They had two daughters, Ethel and Annie, and utilised their front room for the business of Post Office and General Store. Pictured outside this Post Office is milkman Bob Osey, who was employed by Mr. Walter Smith of Sadler's Farm, Lower Pennington Lane.

One Lymington post lady received international recognition. In 1917 Miss Violet Bennett was one of the first women to be employed by the G.P.O., when menfolk were conscripted for First World War duty. Violet learned morse code in order to send messages all over the country, and acted as telegraphist and counter-clerk on alternate weeks. Lymington Post Office stayed open from 8 a.m. till 7 p.m., including Saturdays, staff remaining for a further hour each day to balance the books. Telegraphists also worked from 9-10.30 on Sunday mornings, after which Violet would scurry off to the Catholic Church to play the organ. The staff at the main Post Office in the 1920s comprised head postmaster Mr. Fife, two overseers, three writing clerks, four counter-clerks/telegraphists, and a dozen postmen who delivered the 1d. letters twice daily.

In 1927 one of the clerks lodged with overseer Mr. Tribe. One day Mrs. Tribe chanced to discover a great number of used stamps in the clerk's room – and on investigation, a detective caught the clerk sticking used stamps on to outgoing mail in the sorting office, whilst pocketing the money which had been handed over the counter. He was given instant dismissal. Violet retired in 1949 on a weekly salary of £5, and as Mrs. Violet Loader, appeared in the Guinness Book of Records in 1991 as the oldest practising church organist at the age of 101.

18 · The Lymington Poor House

The system of Workhouses, providing a place of shelter for homeless and poor people in return for work, was established in England in the early 18th century. Lymington Poor House was built in 1738 at the site of the present Infirmary in East Hill, costing £248 10s. Richard Budden was the first Master, with Henry Hackman appointed as the Medical Officer, with salaries of £10 per annum each. One of the overseer's duties was to find apprenticeships for males from 7 to 24 years, and females from 7 to 21 years or marriage, and in 1738 there was a list of 64 people deemed suitable to accept such apprentices. The number of children indentured between 1700 and 1773 was 141.

In 1780 it was agreed that if any inmate from Lymington Poorhouse was seen about the streets not wearing the letters LP for identification, the Master's pay be taken off for the week. And that same year James Alexander was warned that if he did not contribute towards the maintenance of his child, the Parish would endeavour to get him on board a Man o' War ship. By 1788 there were discussions with the neighbouring parishes of Boldre, Brockenhurst and Beaulieu, who organised their own Poor Houses, to combine their resources and build one common Union Workhouse to serve the whole district. Agreement could not be reached until 48 years later, when it was finally decided to build such a Workhouse on the site of the old Poor House, on what was then Union Hill. Mr. Kempthorne was the architect of a building to accommodate 270 inmates, which cost £4,500 to construct in 1836. The Workhouse was surrounded by three acres of grounds where vegetables were cultivated to make the institution as self-supporting as possible. A typical Sunday diet there at that time was – breakfast: ½ lb. of bread with skimmed milk; dinner: 5 oz. dressed mutton with vegetable soup; supper: broth, and there might be a little cheese to follow if the Master desired.

Later renamed as the Lymington Infirmary, the present in-patient wards were constructed in the late 1930s comprising two ground-floor wards and a first-floor maternity ward; the latter facility continued until just after the Second World War. An adjoining Day Hospital complex was built in 1981-82, at a cost of £700,000 inclusive of fittings.

19 · Shipbuilding on Lymington River

In 1667 Charles Guidot sold to John Coombes, shipbuilder, "all that piece of land bounded on the north by Lymington town slip, on the east by the sea or river, and on the west by the King's Highway" – and this 2½ acres has been a shipyard ever since. Up until the early 1800s shipbuilding in Lymington was mainly confined to trading vessels up to about 60-tons, also Revenue Cutters for the Government. Yachting was a comparatively new sport when, in 1821, the Royal Yacht Club (later Squadron) was formed by some 50 members, including Joseph and James Weld. Joseph owned Lulworth Castle in Dorset, but spent six months each year at his Pylewell House, Lymington, where, being a skilful designer, he began building yachts on Pylewell Hard.

In 1819 Thomas Inman sold his small boatbuilding concern at Hastings and brought his family – his wife, three sons and three daughters – in his own sailing boat to Lymington, to start a similar business here. His considerable talent came to the notice of Joseph Weld – and in 1821 Inman built his first boat for Mr. Weld, *The Arrow*. So impressed was the yachtsman with this vessel that the Pylewell Hard industry was transferred to Mr. Inman's Boatyard on Lymington River. Mr. Weld became his most worthy patron, spending £30,000 on the construction of his three famous yachts, *The Arrow*, The *Lulworth* and *The Alarm*, plus £1,200 for annual upkeep.

Fifty-eight years after her launch *The Arrow* was still the most formidable cutter afloat, winning the first Gold Cup at Cowes, the 1826, 1850 and 1852 King's Cup, and the Round the Isle of Wight Race for 100 guineas in 1850. *The Lulworth*, built to Mr. Weld's own design at a cost of over £14,000, won the 1828 King's Cup and Ladies' Cup. Even more successful was *The Alarm*, launched in 1830 as the largest in the cutter class, which won the 1830, 1831, 1832 and 1838 King's Cup at Cowes, before Mr. Weld had the yacht cut in two and lengthened into a 248-ton schooner. She was one of the few English boats to defeat the celebrated *America* which took the Queen's Cup to the United States.

The name *The Alarm* was so revered in Lymington that an inn at the foot of Quay Hill was named after her, also most appropriately the Lymington Corporation's new fire engine in 1928. Many smaller boats were constructed at Inman's Yard, before Thomas Inman retired in 1845 to be succeeded by his son George and his brother James, though soon afterwards James became mentally ill. As the boatyard extended along all the river front between the Quay coalyard and the Sea Water Baths, so George became a prosperous property owner around the area, and was later joined by his son Edwin – but such was their extravagant lifestyle that the firm found itself in the hands of mortgagees. The whole of the Inman estates were sold after the death of Edwin's widow in 1887.

The boatyard subsequently passed into the successive ownership of: the Calcin Brothers; Watkins; Stote (as manager for the mortgagees); Spender Brothers; Ealing, Mellors & Gregg; Stote, again; Lunn Brothers; Courtney & Newhook; George Courtney in 1908; and finally the Berthon Boat Company in 1918. That business had been founded in 1877 by the Rev. E.L. Berthon at Romsey, where he was Vicar of St. Mary's for 32 years. He was the inventor of the screw propeller, and of the first collapsible lifeboat, which was 28′ long with a freeboard of 18″, capable of carrying 75 men – but was only about two feet wide when shut, "so that the problem of the most crowded ship carrying sufficient boats to accommodate every soul on board is solved by this ingenious invention". In 1917 the Berthon Boat Company was purchased by Mr. Henry G. May, and later passed on to his grandson David May, and in turn to great-grandsons Brian and Dominic May. With the addition of a 300-berth marina in 1968, the firm expanded and by 1991 employed a workforce of over 100, building custom luxury yachts, R.N.L.I. Arun-class 52′ lifeboats, and pilot boats.

These pictures show *The Alarm* winning the Royal Thames Yacht Club silver cup on June 25th, 1840, and secondly after she had been lengthened into a 248-ton schooner.

Alarm as a cutter.

Alarm as a schooner.

Lymington shipyard.

20 · Processions and Parades

Every Whit-Sunday practically everyone in Lymington turned out for the Hospital Sunday parade through the town. Young girls were invariably dressed in all-white frocks, hats and stockings for the occasion, whilst little boys were often dressed in sailor suits. This parade must have taken place during the First World War, for behind the Lymington Town Band and local sailors on the left, are around fifty marching New Zealand soldiers, who had been wounded in France and sent back to convalesce at Home Mead in the High Street, converted into a hospital. The Hospital Sunday parade was held to raise funds on which Lymington Hospital relied, and members of the public were pressed to place their coins in collecting tins. Charlie Doe went round with his collecting tin tied to the end of a long pole, from which there was a fabric chute to a receptacle at the bottom, so that people watching the parade from their first-floor windows could make contributions.

The shop on the extreme left, No. 21, was run by H. Bond, confectioner and toy dealer, who curiously has "Ices" and "Chops and Steaks" paper stickers in his windows; next door, No. 22, came Lewis & Badcock the auctioneers and valuers, who proclaim "Furniture removed by Land and Sea", and the premises on the left-hand side of the double wooden gates for the horse-drawn removal waggons was a small office which acted as an agency for The Lymington Gas & Coke Company; No. 23 was the shop of Gauntlett & Prince, advertising Cinderella boots and shoes; whilst No. 24 was occupied by the pharmaceutical chemist G.H. Gare (late Adam U. Allen) who also sold Kodak photographic goods, this shop eventually being acquired by Boots the Chemists. No. 25, High Street, was one of the most popular grocer's in the town, South Hants Stores, where the aroma from freshly ground coffee beans aroused many a nostril, this business later becoming Willis & Son, then in the 1970s Oakshott's, and now Tesco's home and wear department. Next in the picture comes Mr. James Weeks in No. 26, the cutler and umbrella maker; the tall and imposing No. 27 was occupied by Mr. Walter N. Savage, tobacconist and delivery agent, before Nos. 26 and 27 eventually became Rugg's the tobacconists.

Lymington High Street was the route for many processions. Also pictured is the Band of Hope procession on July 19th, 1905, when representatives included the local Baptists and the Wessex division. The children on the right hold aloft a banner which reads: "Strong drink shall be bitter to them that drink it," intended to warn off the town's many drunkards from its 45 inns and ale houses.

BAND OF HOPE PROCESSION. JULY 15. 1905.
HIGH STREET. LYMINGTON.

21 · From Theatre to Laundry to Machine Works

The Pierside Theatre, pictured on the far side of the river, was built by Major Jobling. It was decidedly odd to build an entertainments theatre on such a remote site, though the Major constructed a landing stage for patrons – but it was found this infringed upon the rights of the rowing-boat ferries operating from the Quay, who then took over the Major's pontoon. So it was only about a year or so later that the theatre was closed down, and the building was bought in 1926 by Alfred Walmsley and Edmund Morgan for conversion into the Lymington Model Laundry. The premises, with its five-bedroom cottage in which the two families lived, was acquired from Mrs. Allenby, whose brother was local Alderman Cornish, whilst her brother-in-law was General Allenby of Indian Mutiny fame.

Mrs. Fitzpatrick was manageress in charge of the fifty workers in the laundry, where the ironing ladies operated from the former orchestra stalls – while strings of washing lines were erected at the rear. The laundry possessed two delivery vans, a Model-T Ford and a Wolseley, reaching customers as far distant as Beaulieu and Lyndhurst. Most notable clients included Lord Montagu of Beaulieu, Lady St. Cyres of Walhampton House, Mr. William Whitaker who had 40 servants at Pylewell House, the Hon. Mr. Andress of Elmers Court, and Lady Hamilton-Gordon of Bywater House, who entertained the Italian dictator Mussolini there just before the Second World War. Along the river side of the railway track, the railway men had their allotments.

In 1936 the laundry was sold to Mr. Pigott, who in turn sold the premises in 1958 to Mr. Nelson Ewer, an engineer who employed up to 80 staff making plastic injection moulding machines, presses for Rolls-Royce RB2-11 jet engine blades, etc. He acquired a 1912 10-ton crane from Charles Parsons at Wallsend-on-Tyne, innovator of steam turbine ships, and Mr. Ewer added a factory extension to fit the crane. In the late 1970s he sold the factory, and after various owners was taken over by Green Marine, boatbuilders of lifeboats and round-the-world racing yachts.

The Ferry, Lymington

22 · Lymington Cottage Hospital

In 1912 several people in Lymington, to whom King Edward VII had been known personally, decided a memorial should be set up in his memory. A self-appointed committee agreed a hospital should be built, thus sparing Lymington's 5,000 inhabitants the prospect of travelling to the Royal South Hants Hospital at Southampton, or the Royal Victoria, Boscombe. Under the chairmanship of Lord Arthur Cecil, the committee opened a public subscription list and organised fund-raising events, such as concerts at the Morant Hall, Brockenhurst. Local architect Mr. Benjamin drew up plans for a hospital costing £800, and builders Stone & St. John carried out the work on land donated by the Lord of the Manor, Keppel Pulteney. Florence Nightingale sent a letter of congratulation when the hospital was opened in 1913, comprising two four-bedded wards, male and female, a one-bed emergency ward, operating theatre, X-ray room, dispensary and kitchen. Matron Miss D. Lynch had her sitting room on the ground floor, whilst the other nurse, her sister Miss E. Lynch, had her accommodation on the first floor.

By 1928, with patients rising to 800 a year, £2,200 was raised by collections to enlarge the building by extending the wards and adding a children's ward. That same year a private ward block was built from private funds. When the hospital joined a training scheme for probationer nurses, local people organised a competition so that two plots of land were purchased in King's Park, on which a nurses' home was built for £2,500. Wealthy American visitors Mr. Barkley Henry and his wife Mary were both treated in Lymington Hospital in 1929, and although Mrs. Henry died on her return, her husband presented the hospital with a new theatre, and X-ray and physiotherapy rooms in her memory. That same year £5,000 was raised for new surgical wards and offices.

Two "temporary" hutment wards were added during the 1939 war, with wounded soldiers and prisoners-of-war amongst the patients. In 1980 a £150,000 public appeal was launched for a new casualty unit and pathology block, and trepidations amongst the fund-raising steering committee proved totally unfounded as a staggering £450,000 was realised before Princess Anne formally opened these new additions in 1983. The original hospital, pictured below, now forms the administration offices.

23 · Lymington Golf Club – Victim to the Sea

Members of Lymington Golf Club, pictured in 1934 outside the wood and corrugated-iron clubhouse, just inside the sea wall. The Club was started around the year 1893 with a 12-hole course, all below sea level, but in 1910 it was reduced to nine holes. Said a town guide of the day: "The links are situated about a mile from the town, right on the shores of the Solent, and for salubrity and picturesqueness are unsurpassed. The air is very fine and bracing, and the course is a good sporting one with plenty of natural hazards." In 1915 the Club had a membership of 60, and there were also a ladies' club, playing over the same course as the men, and a Town Golf Club, with a separate club-house. The bogey for the course was 82, and a good many visitors also played there, with the annual Spring Meeting a popular competition.

Alas, one of the course's natural hazards was the sea, and in 1916 a great tidal wave found the sea wall being breached and the Oxey Marsh area flooded, so that Club members were forced to close their course. It was eventually reopened in the mid-1920s, when membership increased to around 200. The committee comprised mostly of businessmen from the town, but the clubhouse was so bleak in the winter that they held their meetings in an upstairs room at the *Londesborough Hotel* in the High Street, where they could also enjoy a hearty supper for 2/6d. With a par 35 for the nine holes, Bill Warwick was the club pro and greenkeeper – and sometimes barman – while Fred Cole, licensee of the nearby *Chequers Inn*, also taught golf there.

The Club kept going until, in 1937, there was another terrible storm, the sea wall was again breached, and the course closed. The last president was Mr. John C. Akerman, of Througham Place, Beaulieu, chairman of Associated Newspapers (which included the "Daily Mail"), who commuted by train daily to his work in London. His wife was also a member of the Lymington Golf Club, and they would arrive by chauffeur-driven Rolls-Royce. In 1938, the year after the flooding, Mr. Akerman summoned secretary George Webb and the remainder of the committee to his Beaulieu mansion, where he gravely intoned that he thought war was imminent, and his suggestion that the Golf Club be closed down met with general, but reluctant, approval.

Seen in this picture outside the clubhouse are (left to right): George Thompson, proprietor of Culls the Drapers, 28 High Street; Freddie Webb, builder; Mr. Gibson, Lymington Gaslight & Coke Co.; Mr. Eddie Cole, solicitor's clerk at Heppenstall's; Mr. Carson timber merchant; Mr. Taylor; Mr. Jack Booth, town registrar and Football Club secretary; Mr. Eric Thompson, son of George; Mr. Eric Thurgood, teller at Lloyd's Bank branch; Mr. Don Dyer builder; Mr. Alfred Isted, director of Ford's in the High Street; Mr. "Iley" Scutt, bank clerk and son of the Lloyd's Bank branch manager; Mr. Frank Robinson, clerk with Wellworthy; Mr. Noel Holtom, cattle dealer and butcher. Seated: Charlie Isted, brother of Alf, director at Ford's.

24 · St. Thomas' Street I

This early photograph of St. Thomas' Street shows, on the extreme right, one of the oldest shops in the town, No. 40, dating from 1620 which became Phyllida the dress shop. The house next door, No. 39, was converted into a fashion shop run by Madame Isabel, who sold American, French and English-made corsets, also motor-caps, hats and veilings for the discerning lady motorist. This shop was later divided into three, with Kew Laundry on the left, a shoe shop on the right, and the "Lymington Times" office in the centre where Mrs. "Dossie" Curry accepted adverts and reports. The shop was afterwards acquired by the Bournemouth Gas Co.

Events in the town had been dutifully recorded in the "Lymington Chronicle" newspaper for 75 years before Mr. Charles Curry snr. founded the "Lymington Times" in April, 1932. He had been made editor of the Canadian Forces' newspaper during the First World War, and went on to serve with the "Daily Express", before restarting the "Christchurch Times" in 1925, then purchasing the "New Milton Advertiser" three years later. But the "Chronicle" did not take kindly to the introduction of the "Lymington Times", so they offered cheap advertising rates and persuaded newsagents not to accept sufficient copies of the "Times". Undeterred, Mr. Curry delivered the 'papers in his Austin 7 car, and employed Sam Bishop to wear billboards and sell his newspapers in the street, though most of his commission was spent in the *Railway Inn* in Station Street. The success of the "Lymington Times" was fully realised when the owners of the "Chronicle", admitting they could no longer run their 'paper at a loss, sold Mr. Curry the "Chronicle" title for £100 – but he was unable to afford a further £100 to purchase 78 years of "Chronicle" files, for in those days £10 would buy a ton of newsprint.

No. 38, Woodmancote, was the residence of Major Gerald Harding, and one of his daughters, married Robert Hole, who lived next door in Heathcote House with an aunt, Miss Herringham; he later founded the Community Association and Sea Scouts' troop.

25 · Lymington's Sea Water Baths

Lymington has long been known for its Sea Water Baths, going back at least as far as the 1780s, using an inlet from the salterns for its source. The proprietress of that day, Mrs. Beeston, advertised her "strengthening sea baths", and there was also Legge's Baths. Terms in 1825 read: "For a warm bath, 3s. 6d.; shower ditto, 2s 0d.; cold water bath with guide, 1s. 0d; ditto without a guide, 6d. Every care and attention to the comforts of the invalid and the convalescent will be found strictly observed". The guide was a man who kept the bathers afloat by use of a rope.

To enhance the town's reputation as a watering place, a public company, the Lymington Bath & Improvement Co., resolved to erect more commodious Baths and enclose a considerable tract of mudland. Almost £6,000 was raised by £25 shares and donations. Architect for the main building, with one wing for use by the ladies, the other by gentlemen, and a circular upper room for social gatherings, was William Bartlett of Lymington. The machinery installed under the direction of civil engineer John Silvester afforded hot, cold or vapour bathing. At the western extremity were the large open-air swimming baths, whilst the adjacent grounds were used for archery and other sports.

But within a few years the Company was in financial difficulties, until Lymington's representatives in Parliament effected a temporary rescue by contributing up to £3,000. This assistance was short-lived, for around 1855 the Baths were sold for as many hundreds of pounds as they had cost in thousands, to Mr. George Inman from the nearby shipyard. His company in turn leased the Baths to the Lymington Sea Baths Co. on Christmas Day, 1886.

But the following year the whole of the considerable Inmans' family estate was sold, owing to their rather extravagant lifestyle, and the Baths were eventually acquired by Mr. A.E. Spender. In 1902 the Baths were auctioned in London, when Mr. T.J.D. Rawlings proved the successful bidder. The Lymington Sea Water Baths were widely advertised as the largest open-air baths along the South Coast, and in 1929 they were taken over by the local Corporation. Thus they have successfully been operated by the Lymington Borough Council, the New Forest District Council, and latterly by Lymington & Pennington Town Council. The old Bath House, pictured, became the headquarters of the Lymington Town Sailing Club on their formation at the end of the Second World War, who lease the premises from the District Council. The floods at the end of December, 1989, left the building flooded to a depth of seven feet. By that time the Sailing Club membership had reached 1,100, and they were afforded one of the finest panoramic views across the Solent from their Solent Room extension to the clubhouse, designed by eminent local architect Roger Pinckney.

26 · The Great Snowstorm of 1908

This photograph was taken during the great snowstorm of April 25th, 1908, when snow eventually accumulated several feet deep throughout the town – and during this blizzard there was a terrible collision in the Solent, between Yarmouth and Lymington, involving H.M.S. Gladiator and the American liner St. Paul. A stagecoach can be seen in the High Street negotiating the hazardous highway.

The shop on the extreme left is No. 84, occupied by Mr. F. Dale, the tailor and habit maker. No. 85 belonged to Mr. A.C. Last, the pastrycook and confectioner, complete with refreshment rooms, who also catered for fetes, banquets, garden and wedding parties. Mr. T. Gray ran his saddlery business from No. 86, whilst Mr. A.E. Woodford's toy shop next door was a favourite for local children. The Music Saloon at No. 88 had been founded in 1789 by George Philip Klitz, a former bandsman in the Flintshire Regiment, who sold pianos and other musical instruments and sheet music; the firm began selling radios in the mid–1920s, and television sets in 1952. The Klitz family were organists at St. Thomas' Church for over half a century: Philip Klitz from 1831-32 when he was appointed organist of All Saints' at Southampton, Charles Klitz then took over as organist at Lymington until he died in 1864, then Robert Augustus Klitz from 1864 until he died in 1887. The large shop occupying Nos. 89 and 90, complete with tall flagpole, was the premises of George F. Saul, who crammed his windows with hardware goods and shotguns, and sold paraffin and petrol in cans. Mr. Saul also kept a shed and garage in Broad Lane to store his paraffin and petrol tanks and a delivery van.

Lymington had also suffered from a great frost, which began on Christmas Day, 1739, and continued until the end of January, 1740. With all trade and work impossible in such extreme temperatures; a bowl of boiling strong punch changed to solid ice within eight minutes, spittle froze before it reached the ground, and bread could not be cut unless placed by a fire for almost an hour. In such dire conditions, the mayor and burgesses called a meeting on January 16th, 1740, "and agreed to distribute to the poor of the parish the sum of ten pounds, on account of the severity of the season of the year, in bread and meat".

27 · Pennington's 13th Century Chapel

The Manor of Pennington was for a great time held in undivided thirds, by three different owners, amongst the earliest being the following lords of the manor: Henry of Thistleden and his successor Henry Peverell in 1285 and 1337 respectively; John Nervett and his successors the Philpotts in 1327, 1485, 1503 and 1531; and John Bole and his successors from 1486 to 1596. In 1803 the estate passed to the Tomline family, and in 1834 it was acquired by John Pulteney. Magdalen Chapel once existed in Pennington, with its earliest mention in 1276, endowed with 60 acres of "priestlands", with the three overlords appointing the priests. Pennington was ecclesiastically part of Milford until 1839, and the first recorded vicar is Walter de Kemeseye (1339-47).

The foundation stone for the first parish church was laid on April 25th, 1838, before a large gathering of spectators, including John Pulteney, lord of the manor, who donated the site of 3 rod, 2 perch, in size. The following March the church, 47'6" long and 20'6" broad, with spirelet and bell, was consecrated by the Bishop of Winchester under the title of St. Mark. The church was furnished with a barrel-organ which could emit two tunes, "The Old Hundredth" and the National Anthem, whilst parishioners provided other instruments for additional arrangements. Along with a gallery, there was seating for around 200.

This church lasted for a mere 20 years, for a faculty was obtained for its demolition and work on the present church began in 1858. During its construction, services were held in the school, specially licensed by the Bishop, the Rt. Rev. Dr. Sumner, who duly consecrated the new St. Mark's on July 25th before a large congregation who contributed an offertory of over £93. Seating around 400, the building cost £2,038, raised by voluntary donations and grants, with the Pulteney family contributing £686. The bell belonged to the first church, and was presented by the Vicar of Milford, the Rev. T. Robinson, as patron. The Parsonage was built in 1846, but the following May the incumbent, the Rev. Lewis Playters Hird, and his only child, four year old Lewis Hawker Hird, both died of malignant fever, and were buried in the same grave in the churchyard.

ST. MARK'S CHURCH, PENNINGTON, HANTS.

28 · The Traders on Lymington Quay

This photograph of Lymington Quay at around 1910 shows the 120′ long paddle-steamer *Lymington*, which was the London & S.W. Railway's first ship for the Lymington–Yarmouth crossing, arriving on service in 1893. Built of steel at Southampton, local passengers enthused over the steamer's plush accommodation: the saloon was upholstered in Utrecht velvet, the decorative ceilings painted in gold and white, and there were wooden panels of maple and oak. She had a certificate to carry 311 passengers.

The shop on the Quay nearest the river was run by Mr. Greenfield, who was also one of the half-penny-ferrymen: he used the premises as a sweets, grocery and swap shop; the rear portion of the property was the store and bottle-cleaning plant of Mr. Mew, the brewer, a prominent Freemason who displayed a large sign of the Masons' regalia on the brick wall. The house next door to the shop was the home of Joseph William Cleall, an employee of Mew Langton. Beyond that is the little *Ship Inn*, which had a six-inch board bedded in clay just inside the front door to combat high tides. Next door was Mr. W. Smith, the baker and shipping supplier, which became a faggot and pea shop. On the end of this row of Quay properties, on the corner with Quay Street, was the *Yacht Inn*, which finally closed down on December 28th, 1911, to become Langley's sweet shop.

The next row of buildings to the right were known as Back Quay, and along the narrow lane between these two rows there was a miniature railway track for trolleys bearing barrels of Mew Langton's ales which had been brought across by boat from their Isle of Wight brewery. The house on the river front with bay window was the home and offices of Mr. Mew. To the right can be seen the offices, stable and coalyard of Mr. John Dimmick, which extended up into Mill Lane. He advertised "Best Seaborne Coals at lowest current prices", and was the sole agent for "The Celebrated Caradoc Coals". The large rounded tree beyond was the site of George Tiller's Nurseries, who specialised in everything horticultural from fruit trees, cabbage plants, flower pots, manures, general gardening work and home grown tomatoes, to wreaths and bridal bouquets "on shortest notice".

29 · Mrs. St. Barbe's School for the Poor

Over the years thousands of Lymington children were educated at this school in New Lane, opposite the Baptist Church, off New Street. The school was opened in 1835, and a large inscribed tablet added later read: "Mrs. Ann St. Barbe, widow of Samuel St. Barbe esqre, of Ridgway, in this parish, during her lifetime gave the site and enclosed it, built the dwelling houses, and contributed largely to the erection of the school rooms. The trustees, since her decease on the 17th June, 1840, have caused this record of her benevolence to be here inscribed." Mrs. St. Barbe had donated £220 for the purchase of the land, about half an acre, and the school was erected for the poor children within the parish and its vicinity, in the principles of the Church of England upon the plan of the National Society for Schools.

The pupils were segregated: the girls occupied classrooms on the left-hand side of the school and were taught by spinsters, whilst the boys on the right-hand side had male teachers. An infants' school was founded in Ashley Lane in 1859, but 29 years later it was sold to become the Foresters' Hall, whilst a new infants' school was erected on the opposite side of New Lane. In 1872 it was agreed that pupils in Standards 4, 5 and 6 should pay 2d. a week for their education instead of 1d., and by this time the school roll had risen to 122. In the winter of 1871 many children were absent with chilblains, but that Christmas Mrs. St. Barbe sent buns for each child. Pupils were given a half-day's holiday in 1893 "on account of a circus being in the town and the procession passes round as the children start school." The school was often closed for diseases: in 1900 for six weeks with scarlet fever; in 1906 for eight weeks because of a diphtheria epidemic; in 1912 for six weeks owing to measles.

Headmaster Mr. Billy Taylor and two teachers were mobilised during the First World War; pupils played their part as the girls raised money to purchase wool for injured soldiers in the Home Mead Hospital in the High Street, whilst the boys collected 6 cwt. of horse chestnuts in a fortnight to provide carbon for gas-mask filters. By 1936 a total of 287 children were taught in eight classes. Children evacuated from Southampton arrived in the 1939 war, when air-raid shelters were excavated in the Emsworth Road playground, along the churchyard wall. In 1947 H.M. Inspectorate reported that, with 392 pupils, the buildings "are old fashioned and unacceptable for modern teaching practice. Negotiations for providing better facilities have been proceeding since March, 1945". The junior school section finally moved to Victory Park, off Avenue Road, in 1972, but it was not until 1991 that the New Lane school finally closed when the infants' school also moved to a new building in the Victory Park grounds.

30 · When Dan Bran Fired at the Ferry

One of Lymington River's greatest characters was Dan Bran, son of George Bran of Woodside, a mariner who sailed on board such famous local yachts as *Alarm* and *Fortuna*. Named Daniel Plat Bran by his mother, after Colonel Platoff who was standing as the local candidate for Parliament at the time, young Dan began a seven-year apprenticeship on March 22nd, 1882, with Edwin Inman at Lymington Shipyard (later Berthon). His indentures stated that "he shall not contract matrimony within the said term nor play at cards or dice tables or any other unlawful games whereby his Master may have any loss with his own goods. He shall not haunt taverns or playhouses." Dan's wages began at 2/- a week for the first year, with annual increments of 2/- until he was paid 14/- for the seventh year. Unable to write, father and son signed the indentures with their own marks.

After working as a spar maker at Poole, Dan began his own boatbuilding business in 1910 in a large wooden shed on the very edge of the river by the sea water baths. He designed and built the first 11' Lymington Pram dinghy in 1912 for keen yachtsman Capt. Nicholson of Creek Cottage, followed by the 14' Pram in 1925. He also built the popular Lymington Scows, still raced today. Dan never resorted to plans to build his boats for, possessing a superb eye, he drew out their contours on the dirt floor of his shed, which proved so precise that any ruler was unnecessary. He would often row his flat-bottomed boat across to Yarmouth, using the tides to their greatest benefit.

Of dishevelled appearance and at times strong odour, Dan and his wife lived in Coastguard Cottage, conveniently next to the Mayflower pub, where Dan was a great benefactor. He once asked landlord Fred Stevenson for a bucket of hot water, in which he proceeded to wash his socks in the bar before placing them by the fireplace to dry; he threw the dirty water out of the pub door into the darkness, straight over a customer about to enter! Dan was often to be seen hunting on the marshes with his 12-bore shotgun. After issuing several warnings to the Southern Railway concerning the excessive speed of their paddle-steamers in the river, Dan's patience was exhausted when the steamer *Solent* caused such a wash as to break the moorings of his dinghies — he straightaway fired both barrels into the canvas around the uncovered wheelhouse. Dan was helped in his boatbuilding by "Buffy" Springer and Bill Gates of Flushards. Dan died in December, 1950, followed by his wife a week later, and the shed and its contents were left to Bill Gates — but the dilapidated building went up in flames one Sunday afternoon in suspicious circumstances, for it did seriously impede the panoramic view across the Solent.

31 · Sunday School Built As Memorial

In 1877 Mr. Francis Crozier, of nearby Delawarr House, built the premises pictured behind these young schoolgirls as a Sunday School for children in the Woodside area. In his grief, Mr. Crozier built the property, complete with little belfry at the top of the eaves, as a memorial to his wife Harriet. He acquired the plot of land from Mr. Samuel Perry for the sum of £10. Summoned by the sound of the bell, children attended their Sunday classes, and other activities were carried on there during the weekday evenings, such as boxing, and around the time of the First World War local lads used the building for their changing room for the Woodside Wonders football team, who were practically unbeatable. The footballers used the little stream which runs along the rear of the property to wash themselves down after their matches in the adjoining field.

In this picture, the house with the laundry washing seen drying on the clothes line was occupied by Mr. "Winkle" Blake, who sold fish around the town from his horse and cart. Occupant in the first of the pair of cottages was spinster Nellie Smoker, with her mother and two brothers, all staunch members of the local Salvation Army, who met on the Woodside Green shown above, singing hymns to the accompaniment of cornets, drums and tambourines, also at their meeting hall in Emsworth Road, later purchased by estate agents for conversion into an auction sales room. In the end cottage above lived Mrs. Woodford and her lodger, painter and decorator Mr. Stubbington.

32 · "Try the Little Shop"

No. 13, High Street, was known as "Pardey's Cheap Hardware Stores", selling three cups and saucers for 6½d., tea plates from 1d. each, dinner plates at 2d. or 3d., enamelled saucepans 6½d. and large tumblers from 1d. "For everything you want – try the little shop", Mr. Pardey implored.

He then sold the business to Edward (Frank) Gearey, who was born at Buckland, Lymington, before being posted abroad with the Army Medical Corps during the First World War. It was at the end of those hostilities that he purchased 13, High Street, which he ran with his wife Dorothy, the former Miss Harrison, who is pictured standing in the shop doorway. They sold all manner of items, coat-hangers, frying pans, tin baths, chamber pots, and garden tools. The couple had three children: Frank junior, Joan and Betty. Frank and Dorothy occupied the premises for four years, delivering paraffin by horse and cart around the town and outlying districts.

Frank then suddenly decided to take up a new life at sea, as a steward on liners sailing out of Southampton – but he was never again seen by the family. Dorothy was left to bring up the children, and they lived in a room at the rear of the *King's Arms* pub in St. Thomas' Street, until they were eventually allocated a new council house in 1929.

No. 13 was then purchased by Mr. Everett, who ran a similar trade from the shop, though he used a large, dark blue motor van when he delivered paraffin and ironmongery over a wide area. The shop has had several owners before being acquired by Buds & Blooms the florists.

33 · The Tallest Tomb in England

One prominent landmark west of Pennington is Peterson's Tower, clearly visible to ships out in the English Channel. Mr. Andrew Thomas Turton Peterson was a native of Wakefield, Yorkshire, a descendant of the Philosopher Michele, whose intellectual efforts did much to lead up to the discoveries of Sir Isaac Newton in the 17th-century. Like many boys of that time, Andrew ran away from school to become a sailor, but after a rapid rise through the ranks, was struck down with a serious illness in India. On medical advice he returned to England to study for the Bar, which led to a highly successful career as a barrister. Returning to India, he rose to become leader of the Calcutta Bar, and was for a while Judge of the High Court of Calcutta.

Retiring around 1868, Mr. Peterson settled at "Drumduan", later known as "Arnewood Towers", in the parish of Hordle, just beyond Pennington. There he devoted his time to intellectual and practical pursuits, and as a student of psychology, was a pioneer in the phenomena of Spiritualism, reducing these to law and order with his writings translated into many languages. A great traveller, he had studied the materials and methods of construction used in many lands, and shrewdly foresaw the prominent part Portland Cement Concrete would play in future buildings. On settling at "Drumduan", he immediately began experimenting with concrete and, with many men out of work after the construction of the railway, he was soon the largest employer of labour in the district, raising wages above the low level of that time, and reducing the local Poor Rate by 10d. in the £. Designing and supervising work on the Tower; it is built in a square of 22 feet, with 2' thick walls at the base tapering to 1' thick at the top. On the north side is incorporated an octagonal tower in a 9' circle, with a spiral staircase of 330 steps providing access to the eleven rooms in the main Tower, which rises to 218 feet, with views to Spithead in the east and Poole Harbour to the west. It has withstood all weathers for well over 100 years, including being struck by lightning before the First World War. In 1906 Mr. Peterson died at the age of 92, and an urn bearing his mortal remains was lowered into the crypt beneath the Tower by his elderly remaining workmen, making it the tallest tomb in England.

Peterson's Tower, Sway.

34 · Discovery of a 15th Century House

In 1989 the Lymington builders Colten, whilst renovating the vacant shop at No. 26, High Street, inadvertently made the most surprising discovery by uncovering the remains of the original 15th-Century house which stood on that site – a most important find. The Georgians had built a brick facade in front of the old timber framework and wattle and daub walls – interwoven sticks and mud. The medieval building was 18' wide, with a gable end on to the High Street, and three inter-connecting bays stretched back 25', with a curved archway left open into the roof space to form a most imposing room. The box-framed house had a jetty over the High Street, as the first floor protruded 18" over the front of the ground floor in cantilever fashion. The Georgians' brick facade was built 3' in front of the original ground floor, and thus 18" in front of the first floor. On one of the ceiling beams the builders found two tiny children's shoes, 4½" long, one from the 17th-18th Century, and the other 18th-19th Century. Other discoveries included a mummified bat, and thousands of hazel nuts deposited by mice over the centuries. This is the oldest known house to survive in the town.

This picture shows the shop in 1915, with Fred Weeks standing in the doorway. His sister Ada was born in the flat over the shop in 1866, the daughter of James and Eliza Weeks. She married Charlie Berry, a painter and decorator from Milford who worked for Elgar's in the High Street from the age of 18 until he retired at 65. Fred Weeks and his sister Maude helped run the shop before the business moved across the road to No. 101, High Street in 1927. The photograph shows the wide range of goods supplied by Weeks: cutler and umbrella maker, walking sticks sold for 4d., or for 1/- if they had bone handles, spectacles "for defects of the sight", and sunshades which Maude made up from customers' own materials. Fred died in 1956 in his seventies; he was survived by a niece Dorothy, who spent many hours as a young girl peering from the window over the shop, watching waiters and waitresses serving teas to customers seated on the balcony of the *Angel Hotel* on the opposite side of the road. In 1915 the shop next door, No. 27, was run by Charlie Savage the tobacconist, later taken over by Rugg's, who expanded by converting 26 and 27 into one shop.

35 · Shell Demolished Outside Loo!

The *Chequers Inn* at Woodside, Lymington, on December 18th, 1914. That date was left imprinted in the memory of the licensee of the day, Mr. Fred Cole, for a shell from a British gun at Fort Victoria ricocheted through the inn, passing down through the roof of the building, then striking an out-house used as a beer store which had been converted from old stables. The shell then struck the rear of the cottage next door, demolishing the outside lavatory. Bill Dyer the bricklayer and his family who lived there found this most inconvenient!

Standing at the top of the ladder in the photograph is licensee Mr. Cole, who had run the *Red Lion* in the High Street before obtaining a transfer to the *Chequers* in 1910, which he continued to run with his wife Jo until 1947. At the time of the shelling she was reclining quietly in an upstairs bedroom, having just given birth to son Maurice. On Fred's death another son, Eddie Cole, ran the pub for a short while, before continuing as a solicitor's clerk at Heppenstall's in the High Street.

The *Chequers Inn* was at one time the Customs Office for the salt or Exchequer office, with its close proximity to the row of salt pans which stretched along the coastline between Lymington and Keyhaven. Documented deeds for the *Chequers* site date back to 1695, detailing a 999-year lease between Eleanor Pierce and John Guyer. In 1750 ownership of the property passed from John and Betty Brent to John and Thomas Elgar. Landlord in 1791 was James Viney. The sign of The Chequers is probably one of the oldest in the world, since a chequer sign was found during the excavation of the ruins of Pompeii.

36 · Lymington's T.T. Motor-Cycle Racer

Cecil Barrow acted as chauffeur to the Earl of Egmont at Avon Castle until, following his marriage at Ringwood in 1919, he came to Lymington to start his own life as a motor-cycle and cycle dealer. Before he was allowed to purchase Mr. H.T. Bath's corn and seed merchant's shops at 79 and 80, High Street, his father Harry Barrow first sat in Lloyd's Bank for an hour to gauge the wealth of the townsfolk. Cecil competed in the Isle of Man T.T. races each year from 1925 to '35, finishing second in 1928 at an average speed of 58.92 m.p.h. on a Royal Enfield in the junior class. He practised across Beaulieu Heath, with his daughters acting as timekeepers. Cecil was captain of Southampton speedway team from 1928 to '30, and also raced at Brooklands and Crystal Palace.

Along with Mr. R. Mason and Mr. H. Jones, Cecil featured in a syndicate which built JMB three-wheeled cars, with a 497 c.c. J.A.P. motor-cycle engine laid horizontally below the seat, with chain transmission, and a fabric body over an ash wood frame. Selling for £75 10s. in standard form or £83 10s. for the de luxe, the machine received a good reception from the motoring Press. Around 100 were manufactured until, in 1936, a reduction in taxation of low horsepower four-wheeled cars put paid to the big tax advantage previously enjoyed by the three-wheelers. Cecil added radio sales and repairs to his High Street business, and installed a BP petrol pump – with the storage tank sited beneath the shop floor! A founder-member of Lymington Motor-Cycle Club, Cecil acted as a Home Guard dispatch-rider during the Second World War, delivering messages in record time.

This picture shows Cecil second left, and continuing to the right are mechanics Stan Botting, Midge Haines, book-keeper Miss Payne, Jack Shepherd and Alf Collins. On the extreme left is Mr. Muller, a German motor-cycle enthusiast who lived in a cottage by the *Chequers Inn* and became a close friend of Cecil. Mr. Muller was a scientist and inventor, who experimented with rockets to fire postal mail across the Solent to the Isle of Wight. Alas, the rockets fell short into the sea. Immediately before the war Mr. Muller suddenly disappeared, leaving locals wondering whether he was a spy – although Pathe Gazette film of his rocket-mail was shown at the Lyric Cinema in the town. In 1951 Cecil Barrow's shop was sold to Woolworth's, along with Rowland Hill's the grocer's next door.

37 · Lymington Temperance Band

This is the bandstand which stood on the Bath Road recreation ground, where Lymington Military Band gave regular Sunday concerts. To the left can be seen the tow-boat *Carrier*, which towed barges containing motor vehicles, carts and animals between Lymington and the Isle of Wight. On the extreme right is the old Coastguard House, before Lymington Council transferred the lease to the Lymington River Sailing Club in 1923. Around the time of the Second World War the bandstand suddenly disappeared, and its final destination remained a mystery.

Lymington Band has a long and proud tradition, dating back to its formation in 1883, with an uninterrupted history despite two world wars. Its beginnings resulted from a meeting on the evening of January 1st, 1883, in the Anglesea Temperance Hotel on the corner of Queen Street and Stanford Road, when twelve musical enthusiasts discussed the idea of setting up a band. With the hotel proprietor Mr. W. Batts a principal benefactor, the bandsmen held their first practice in Pardey's Dairy off Lower Buckland Road, then in a room at the Sea Water Baths.

The bandsmen were rewarded with a silver cup and a £10 prize on entering their first competition, at Aldershot, and they joined the Volunteers attached to the Hampshire Regiment. The Band often played at Newlands Manor, Everton, where the Prince of Wales – later to become King Edward VII – was a regular intimate visitor to Mrs. Cornwallis-West. The Prince thought the title of Lymington Temperance Band a huge joke – yet in reality the bandsmen were all abstainers at that time. They also played before the German Emperor, and received his commendation. The Band was never out of the prize list during its first eighty years' existence, won several trophies at Crystal Palace, and competed as far distant as Wales. Their first bandmaster was Mr. Frank Haskell, and relying on voluntary subscriptions for their dependence, their promenade concerts and open-air dances in the town afforded recreation to many listeners during the summer months. The Band also played at other large houses, such as Wainsford where, at splendid skating carnivals, they performed from a bandstand in the middle of the lake, with the grounds illuminated by Chinese lanterns, tar barrels blazed, and a sheep was roasted.

38 · The H.M.S. Gladiator Disaster

On April 25th, 1908, a snow blizzard struck Lymington, which led to a maritime disaster off Yarmouth. The 5,750-ton Royal Navy cruiser H.M.S. *Gladiator*, with 250 men on board, left Portland to steam to Portsmouth in a strong north-west wind and frequent snow squalls. At the same time the American express mail liner *St. Paul* set off from Southampton down the western Solent bound for New York. A big ship of 11,630 tons, the *St. Paul* reduced to half speed as visibility worsened off Yarmouth. The two ships were blanketed in the thick driven snow, and were less than half a mile apart when the look-outs realised they were on collision course, with the *Gladiator* travelling at nine knots and the *St. Paul* at 13 knots.

It needed prompt action by the men on the bridges to obey the general rule in such a situation, to swing the helm hard to port. Capt. Passow on the *St. Paul* correctly followed this procedure after ordering his engines to stop. The *Gladiator*'s navigation officer Lieutenant Mainguy ordered the helm Port-10, but when both ships' sirens were sounded almost simultaneously, the officers on the *Gladiator*'s bridge believed the *St. Paul* had blasted twice, the signal for going to port. Mainguy ordered the *Gladiator* to starboard, but when the bows of the *St. Paul* were heading for the cruiser's side, so the warship's Captain Lumsden shouted "Hard a Port". Alas his order came too late, for the liner's great bow crashed into the *Gladiator* amidships, directly into the mess room, killing several men. Many others were injured, stokers buried under coal, and the remainder thrown clean across the ship. Lumsden called on the *St. Paul* to back off, and the icy waters flooded into the warship. The *Gladiator* keeled over on to her damaged starboard side, and around fifty crew attempted to swim the 250 yards to the Island, whilst the rest crowded on to the ship's upturned hull. The *St. Paul*'s port lifeboats in the lee of the blizzard were iced up and took 20 minutes to free. Soldiers from the nearby Royal Engineers garrison at Fort Victoria gallantly waded to the aid of the sailors swimming ashore, whilst the *St. Paul* evacuated the remainder with Capt. Lumsden finally brought ashore an hour after the collision.

Next day he had to report one Lieutenant and 28 men dead, mostly drowned and swept away by the tide. It took the salvors five months to strip the *Gladiator* of her armaments and eventually raising the hull, an operation which cost £50,000 – yet she was of no further use and was sold to a breaker for £15,125. By a strange quirk of fate, ten years later to the day, April 25th, 1918, the *St. Paul* inexplicably capsized and sank whilst at anchor in New York harbour.

39 · Joseph Diamond the Waggon Builder

The old roadside *Crown Inn* at Buckland, a few yards from the ancient turnpike tollgate cottage which marked the northern entrance to Lymington, where the keeper in 1795 was James Stanley. The cottage was habited until 1952, and dug up in its grounds was an Isle of Wight halfpenny coin dated 1792 bearing the head of Robert Bruce Wilkins. On August 16th, 1764, the town's Freemasons' Lodge was founded at the *Crown*. By 1877 the pub had become known as *The Monkey House* as landlord Stephen Harris kept pet monkeys there, which had the habit of stealing from customers' pockets. It has since been renamed *The Tollhouse Inn*.

Pictured on the right are two of the many horse-drawn waggons, carts and vans made by Joseph Osmond Diamond. He arrived in Lymington from Dorset in 1856 to set up his workshop in Avenue Road, opposite *The Borough Arms*. There he ran his business as a cart and waggon builder, wheelwright, and undertaker. Before the turn of the century he moved to larger premises at nearby 10 and 11, Lower Buckland Road; son Charles took over before Joseph retired in 1920 to live in Fibbards Road, Brockenhurst, where he died eight years later.

Manufacturing all manner of commercial and private horse-drawn vehicles, Charles employed two coachsmiths, two coachbuilders and two coach-painters, any of whom acted as coffin bearers when required. Charles' two sons entered the family business at the age of 14, Eric in 1915 and Ken in 1923. The firm built a new horse-drawn hearse in the mid-1920s, although mourners were charged less if the coffin was pushed to church on a wheeled bier. Charles died on Christmas Day, 1933, and the business was bequeathed to Ken.

Eventually a Sunbeam motor hearse was hired until 1934, when Diamond's purchased their own Daimler sleeve-valve R130 model, with a new coachwork body on a 1928 chassis. This was replaced at the end of the war by a DE27 Daimler with pre-selector gearbox, converted from a large saloon car. A new 4.2-litre Jaguar-engined Daimler was bought for £6,000 in 1971, and in addition to covering a large local area, funerals were arranged and conducted as far afield as Inverness in Scotland to Penzance in Cornwall. Though Eric went totally blind, he continued to make coffins and clean the hearse until he died, shortly before Ken retired in 1976 – which marked the end of the Diamond family connection with the firm.

40 · The Shop Demolished for Road Widening

This shop at the foot of town hill, No. 139, High Street, was demolished not long after this photograph was taken in 1902, in order to widen the junction with Gosport Street. The shop belonged to F. & W. Giddon, the saddlers, before Mr. Pearce ran a china business there for a short while. Next door, No. 138, was the fishmonger's shop which Mr. Eli Rickman had run for over half a century, with his fish displayed in the baskets seen on the pavement outside. Later, Mrs. Balls ran these premises as a men's and boys' outfitters.

The poster to the left of the shop door advertises the musical "My Soldier Boy" to be shown at the Literary Institute, New Street, in February, 1902. It was about 1832 that a literary society was formed in Lymington, but it lapsed after a mere two years. However, it was re-formed in 1846, when the Society purchased a spacious building in New Lane (later New Street) which had previously been used as a theatre since 1771. A new Literary Institute was constructed on the site in 1847, which offered a social meeting place, especially for military officers who were stationed in the town for many years.

On February 5th, 1847, as a result of the County Court Act of the previous year, it was agreed to allow the judge to use the town hall free of charge. The court was later moved to the Literary Institute, where the petty sessions of Lymington rural district were held until the 1920s. The Institute's main lecture hall was enlarged in 1901 to seat 400 persons, there were billiards and reading rooms, with a library containing around 1,250 volumes. The new 1901 "Victoria Wing", in memory of the late Queen, was used exclusively for ladies, with a very comfortable suite of rooms to provide means of social intercourse and recreation. Thus the Institute, by catering for the requirements of both sexes, came to be regarded as one of the principal centres of social life in the town, with various societies making it their headquarters. Lymington Town Band began using these premises for their practice nights soon after their formation in 1883, and continue this tradition today.

41 · Colonel Rooke the Benefactor

The extensive Woodside Gardens property was bought by William Rooke, born in 1747, who married Marianne, sister of Sir Harry Burrard Neale. William died at Woodside on August 6th, 1831, one year after he had purchased that property – the first of the Woodside Rookes. His son, William Wowen Rooke, was born on April 27th, 1804, and became an officer in the 2nd Life Guards before he died at Woodside on April 8th, 1883. A marble drinking fountain was erected in his memory at the western end of St. Thomas' Street, close to its junction with Belmore Lane, in March, 1885.

He left two sons, Colonel Henry Rooke, born at Woodside on May 2nd, 1842, and Captain Algernon Wowen Rooke, of the 84th Regiment, born on August 27th, 1845. Both remained bachelors, and lived with their spinster sisters, Miss Persis Rooke and Miss Mary Rooke, in the imposing Woodside House with its seven acres of grounds. The family owned most of the properties within the Woodside community, and were greatly respected by their tenants, many of whom were of humble origin. The Rookes employed six indoor staff, led by Mr. Fish the butler, and six outdoor staff, under Mr. Hall, the head gardener, and Mr. Herbert Fudge, who was responsible for the horses and tack. Miss Persis rode around in a basket-chair cart drawn by a small Shetland pony. Every Christmas she would personally visit each tenant to distribute ½lb of tea, 2lbs of sugar, and ensure that the coalman, following behind with his horse and cart, off-loaded 2 cwt of coal at each household. Mr. Fudge, who lived in a cottage on the estate, regularly called on the tenants for their 2/6d weekly rents.

Col. Rooke kept his landscaped gardens in fine order, and the grounds were opened to the public on one Sunday each month. Often some 300 adults and children availed themselves of this gesture, strolling around the flower-beds, listening to the Town Band, and enjoying tea and cakes provided by the Colonel. Summer fetes were also staged there. Being a keen horticulturist, Col. Rooke returned from abroad with a rare cymbidium orchid – which he prized so greatly that, when it was in bloom, the greenhouse remained locked to the public. He also kept a few monkeys, which were tethered in the gardens for visitors' amusement. Col. Rooke is pictured on the left with his brother Capt. Algernon and their sisters, taking afternoon tea outside the house. The Colonel was the benefactor who left the fine house and grounds to Lymington Corporation in the mid-1920s, but thirty years later the house, by then in a thoroughly dilapidated and dangerous state, was demolished.

The marble fountain, later resited to Bath Road recreation ground.

42 · When Baptists Were "Dippers"

Lymington Baptist Church was founded in 1688, though its followers met secretly before that date as a persecuted people. They had congregated furtively in one another's homes, fearful of arrest, and these hardy souls were baptised by total immersion at Hatchett Pond, near Beaulieu – hence their nickname "The Dippers". In 1688 they were able to worship openly in a house "fitted up for the purpose on the left-hand side" of South Street (now Captain's Row). When the Baptists decided to build their own church on the present site in New Lane (now New Street) in 1769, their Pastor, the Rev. Joshua Thomas, travelled to London to seek funds. Deciding to make an additional call at Portsmouth on his return journey to add to the considerable monies he had raised, Mr. Thomas had the misfortune to sleep in a damp bed and died there of a severe cold – so his remains were brought back for a funeral service in the new church.

In 1791 there was dissension within this church, so seven members departed to create a second Baptist place of worship in the town, at an old-established ironmonger's on the corner of High Street and New Lane. Mr. William Mursell preached there, but eventually the two factions were reunited – and Mr. Mursell went on to preach at the benighted village of Sway, where the Gospel had not reached, and folk there built a chapel with their own hands. In 1834 the original Lymington church was demolished and, using the old materials, the present more commodious one was constructed at a cost of £1,625, of which legacies amounted to £1,275, leaving only £350 outstanding. The building included a day-school in the rooms below, accommodating 140 scholars – but the following year the National School was opened on the opposite side of New Lane, so the Baptist school closed. In 1883 Robert Wheeler bequeathed the magnanimous gift of £10,000 to support the church's future ministers and indigenous members. A total of 150 souls were interred in the adjoining burial ground, before it was closed by Home Office decree in 1859 – and in 1976 those grounds were levelled to form a car park.

Lymington United Reformed Church was built in 1847 on the High Street site which was once the dwelling house of Thomas Thirle, one of the last barber-surgeons, who used to perform all the bleeding in the town. However, as Presbyterians, they were formed for worship long before that time, one date offered being 1700. They gathered at 31/32, St. Thomas' Street, which was named Old Town Meeting. The present (then Congregational) church, along with schoolrooms to the rear and the adjoining parsonage, were built for £4,500 – and one elderly lady, Mrs. Barham, went round collecting 1d. a month subscriptions which realised an amazing £116 10s. over six years. By 1901 the church had 168 Sunday School scholars and 81 Band of Hope members. In 1972 the Congregationalists became known as the United Reformed Church.

This photograph shows the 1949 Sunday School anniversary at the Baptist Church, with the minister, the Rev. Ernest Camble, standing centre rear. The piped organ was purchased second-hand from Farnham Congregational Church in 1906.

43 · Lymington's Horse-Drawn Fire Service

This fine body of men comprised Lymington Fire Brigade, pictured just after the turn of the century complete with their 1897 horse-drawn hand-pump fire engine. The fire station in those days was situated by the huge water tower near the entrance to the Sports Ground – where these firemen are photographed in front of the old cricket pavilion which was, ironically, destroyed by arson. The identity of all but one of these firemen is known, left to right, back row: Moorcraft, Crouch; middle row: ?, Teague, Adams, Harding; front row: Parker, Hurford, Knewitz, Joyce, Thomas.

At that time Lymington Fire Brigade had its own rules, which declared: "The Fire Brigade shall consist of 15 members or more and called the Borough of Lymington Fire Brigade, such members to hold office at the will of the Council." There was one drill each month without pay, "and any members absent without satisfactory reason shall be fined 6d., and any member who is absent from two drills or two fires a year, without satisfactory reason, shall be dismissed". The fire superintendent and deputy superintendent were appointed by the Council. When attending a fire, the members were paid 2/6d. for the first hour and 1/- for each subsequent hour; bystanders selected to aid the Brigade received 6d. an hour.

The two horses which hauled the fire engine were stabled in the *Angel Hotel* yard. When the large bell on the top of the water tower was rung to summon the firemen to duty, Frederick "Tammy" Neal, the pony-boy and boot-boy at the *Angel*, unlatched the stable doors – and whilst one horse raced to the fire station on its own through the churchyard and The Tins, Tammy rode the other around the High Street and Queen Street. He went on to become cellar-man and garage-man at the *Angel*, and had the privilege of driving the first motor-bus in the town, a Stout made in Salisbury for Mr. Backhurst, who garaged his horse and motor coaches in the *Angel* yard. The troublesome Stout repeatedly broke down, and was replaced by Daimler buses. In 1929 Tammy was made redundant at the *Angel*, but his employer Mr. J. Dickinson wrote glowing references: "He is an honest and sober chap, can drive well, and can clean a car second to none." Tammy spent the remainder of his working life at Dawson's Garage.

In 1919, Lymington Borough Council replaced the hand-pump with a horse-drawn Shand Mason steam fire engine, which had been purchased new by the Bournemouth Corporation in 1900. This appliance could provide two fire-fighting jets of water at a pressure of 100 lbs. per square inch within five minutes of turnout, and burned 28 lbs. of steam coal each working hour. This machine continued in service until replaced by a motorised fire engine in 1928, which the Council named *The Alarm* after Col. Weld's famous yacht. Lymington's Auxiliary Fire Service, with Tammy Neal as driver, rendered invaluable service in the Southampton blitz during the Second World War – though there was some embarrassment when they valiantly fought to retrieve a body which turned out to be a shop window dummy!

The firemen moved from their Southampton Road premises to a new station in Avenue Road, next to the town hall, in 1969.

44 · The Administration of Lymington River

With no proper river wall, the banks being shored up with timber, Lymington River often flooded over the recreation ground area and into houses situated along Bath Road. Rather than make frequent complaints to the local Corporation, the inhabitants along the road – generally amongst the less privileged members of the community, or newcomers to the area – were resigned to such hazards as part of the privilege of living on such a site. One serious flooding occurred in 1909, when the banks were breached by a double tide, and the water rose to a height of eight feet inside the houses. Boards were placed around the walls of these properties in an attempt to keep out the salt, and householders spent days confined to their upstairs rooms. Neighbours rallied round to support one another, with food supplies and other necessities arriving by rowing-boat.

Just beyond the baby's pram in this picture is a stile, over which members of the public could pass and continue along the riverside walk in the foreground, passing in front of the Shipyard and on towards the Quay, to emerge at a five-barred wooden gate next to the electricity power station in Bath Road, practically opposite the junction with Nelson Place. However, this section of the pleasant river walk, between the stile and Nelson Place, was lost to public use when the Berthon Boat Company extended its confines by claiming this right-of-way under the Defence of the Realm Act, 1939, when they constructed ships for the Royal Navy during the Second World War. In 1956 Lymington Borough Council did seek the restitution of this section of the public footpath, but the judge said "it would serve no useful purpose".

There were comparatively few moorings along the river at the time of this picture. Before 1951, the river was administered by Lymington Borough Council, who appointed a River Committee. The growth of yachting in the river, along with its attendant need to finance dredging and other maintenance work, led to the application for a Parliamentary Order to set up a statutory body in order that these expenses did not fall on the general ratepayers in the Borough. So an Act was drawn up for the river to be administered by thirteen Harbour Commissioners, to include two yacht owners who held moorings there, along with representatives of other interested bodies, such as the fishermen and the ferry operators, also the Council.

487B. Recreation Ground, Lymington.

45 · St. Thomas' Street II

St. Thomas' Street, photographed around the time of the First World War. On the extreme right is the *King's Arms*, where the licensee, Mr. J. Buckle, not only sold Mew Langton's ales, but also offered stabling facilities and acted as furniture remover. Next door, the elderly Miss Cole ran her confectionery shop. Then came No. 13, the butcher's shop of Mr. Sid Prichard, a diminutive man who shuffled around the sawdust covered floor, invariably wearing a straw boater hat; in 1948 Mr. Fred Butcher, who had acted as manager of W.R. Fletcher's butcher's business near the foot of the town hill since 1921, purchased Mr. Prichard's concern and continued working there until the age of 80, to be followed by son Doug and grandson Michael. Next door to Mr. Prichard came Mr. Freddie Loader's clock and watch repairing business, with its dark and dismal interior. In No. 11, Alderman Johnnie Gibson operated his newsagent's shop, assisted by his wife, who was the sister of Miss Cole. Next door, the Dawson brothers ran their South Coast Garages, with car sales and repairs. This was followed by the high class tailors of John Jenvey & Sons in No. 9, who dressed wealthy male and female clients in the area. The next two properties were private houses, while Mr. Bates took over No. 6 for his drapery and upholstery business after Mr. Herbert

Rand had vacated that premises and moved down to the High Street, on the corner with Ashley Lane. Mr. Charlie Fry sold cold meats and provisions in No. 5, before it became a bakery. The plot of land next door, an open grassed area with a wooden shed at the rear, was a favourite site for open-air dances before the Lyric Cinema was built there in 1913. Quadrille Court is the imposing house to be seen beyond, named after a card game played there by French officers during the French Revolution.

On the extreme left of the picture, a lady can be seen walking past the upholstery and undertaker's shop of Mr. Frederick William House at No. 33. The garage premises next door was occupied by the South Coast Paint Company, who mixed their own paints there, whilst upstairs Miss Banks ran her private school. She probably frowned on the activities of the next occupant, No. 35, the bookmaker's shop of Mr. Charles E. Nipper, who later moved to rooms in Southampton Road. Above Mr. Nipper's shop, Mr. Bevir the architect operated. This was followed by two large private residences, Heathcote House occupied by Miss May Herringham, and Woodmancote, the home of Major Gerald Harding, from where his eldest daughter Dorothy was married to Mr. Robert Hole, who subsequently founded the Lymington Community Association.

46 · Soup Kitchen for Pennington Schoolchildren

A 1919 photograph of Pennington School, a fine Victorian building in the Village Square. Headmaster was Mr. "Skip" Pattendon, a very strict man, who once caned the entire class of 30 pupils on their right hands to make sure he had punished the culprit of one misdemeanour. The schoolchildren used to sing a rhyme, though not within his hearing: "Skipper Pattendon is a good man, He tries to teach us all he can, To reading, writing and arithmetic, And he don't forget to give us the stick, When he does he makes us dance, Out of England and into France, Out of France and into Spain, Over the hills and back again." The other teachers at the school were his wife Mrs. Pattendon, who also taught needlework, and Mrs. Flossie Torah, with knitting amongst her subjects. Children aged seven to fourteen attended this school, whilst those of five and six years received their education at the infants' school a short distance to the south.

The children eagerly looked forward to the weekly soup kitchen, in a house bearing the date 1897 a little way along Wainsford Road. Miss Helen Fullerton, of Pennington Chase, generously provided the ingredients, whilst volunteer helpers prepared the soup in a large boiler in the kitchen. The hot soup would contain rabbit, peas and the like, and the children would bring their own basin, spoon and bread; they would sit on benches inside the house to eat their soup, which saved them walking home at the middle of the day. Anyone in the village could go along for the soup, and women would collect it in large wash-basins or jugs, and be charged 2d. a quart. The schoolchildren could also subscribe to a penny-a-week club at the school, which they had to save – for this money could only be drawn out when they left school at the age of 14.

The house on the extreme left of this picture belonged to Mr. Galpin, the verger at nearby St. Mark's Church for a great many years; he also undertook shoe repairs in a room at the rear of the house.

47 · Woodside Wonders' Football Club

This is the Woodside Wonders football team, pictured in 1910 proudly displaying their silver cup. They played their home matches in a paddock opposite the *Fisherman's Rest* pub at Woodside, and were almost invincible, such was their great playing record. They used the old Sunday School building on the corner of All Saints' Road and Belmore Lane – which had been built in 1877 by Mr. Francis Crozier as a memorial to his wife Harriet – as a changing room. The footballers are seen at the rear of the Sunday School, and behind the line of trees runs a brook in which they washed themselves down after matches. Young people in the vicinity met in the Sunday School building on weekday evening for many activities, including boxing – which they were taught by a nun, Sister Martin, who would glove up and show the lads the correct way to land a punch and defend themselves.

Seen sitting in the centre of the photograph, with a football between his legs, is Mr. Billy Taylor, the popular headmaster of the National School off New Street, which in those days was sectioned off into two halves, with the girls taught in one section with spinsters as their teachers, whilst the boys occupied the other half with male teachers. Sitting on the left is Fred "Digger" Hayter, who became a seaman on square-rigged ships. He once had the misfortune to slip from the topmast and fall into the sea, a frightening experience which, after being hauled out of the yawning deep, left him so mentally disturbed that he was placed in solitary confinement for two weeks before he was able to regain his composure.

The Woodside Wonders were still functioning after the First World War, and most of those in this photograph can still be identified. They are, left to right, back row: William Gates, a fireman when Lymington's steam fire engine was drawn by two horses; Lot Broomfield, a painter and decorator; the Rev. Charles Bostock senior, later to be succeeded by his son Charles junior as Vicar of Lymington; Jack Cave, also a fireman, who worked for Lymington Borough Council; Dick Freeman, a gardener; Fred "Touchy" Lane, who was employed by Rashley's the builders; Will Hayter; (?); Jack Hayter, a gardener who tended the grounds of nearby All Saints' Church; the Rev. Mr. Points, curate; Arthur Gates, who worked for the old A.G.W.I. oil refinery at Fawley. Front row: Fred Hayter, builder; Fred Cooper; Bill Taylor the headmaster; (?); Harold Taylor, the headmaster's son. Seated: Mr. Len "Honky" Hoare, a pupil who continued as a teacher at the National School; and Dick Taylor, the headmaster's other son.

48 · Started Clothing Mart After Honeymoon

On April 15th, 1872, the marriage took place in Dover between 28 year old George Elliott and Miss Elizabeth Decent, four years his senior. Following a brief four-day honeymoon, the newlyweds travelled to Lymington where, on April 19th, they opened the Lymington Clothing Mart at 87, High Street – now the Gas Co. showrooms. The couple began the business with just £225 in cash; their rent for the premises was £7 a quarter, and they sold three pairs of men's trousers for 5/11d. A busy trade necessitated the move in 1890 to larger premises across the High Street, expanding to Nos. 44-46. Elizabeth died three years later, by which time son Edward had joined the business on an annual salary of £25. Tailoring and shoe repairing was executed on the premises "for ready cash only".

Further prosperity led to Elliott's opening branches at Lyndhurst, Freshwater on the Isle of Wight, Highcliffe, New Milton and Christchurch. In the meantime Edward had married in 1904, but ten years afterwards he was called up for First World War duty as a Captain in the Hampshire Regiment, leaving his father without family support in the business. Towards the end of the war, a daughter Enid (Peggy) was born to the young Elliotts. Edward was adamant that neither his wife nor his daughter should conde-scend to any involvement in the family's trading affairs; in fact Peggy became a competent 'cellist and pianist, appearing in local concerts and on B.B.C. radio's "Children's Hour". Edward was an enthusiastic bellringer at St. Thomas' Church, where his father had served as churchwarden.

In 1939 Peggy was married at Beaulieu Abbey church to Captain John Deighton, of the Royal Tank Corps. Shortly after the outbreak of war he was taken prisoner by the Germans, and spent a whole year in chains during his incarceration. As the Lymington shop became short-handed owing to the hostilities, so Peggy fulfilled her ambition by playing a useful part in the family business. Recovering from ill health, the result of his deprivations, Capt. Deighton retired from the Army in 1947 to join his father-in-law, who died the following year. The Deightons took control, and when their 15 year old daughter Jenny went on an exchange visit to Germany, she made an acquaintance there with Uli Welker, leading to their marriage. Subsequently they took over the running of the business, which was eventually confined to the Lymington premises. This photograph shows the founder, George Elliott, after moving his shop to the southern side of the High Street in 1890.

49 · Churchyard became High Street

"Lymington has all the qualities which characterise a successful health resort. Its climatic conditions are delightful at almost any time of the year, the air being dry and invigorating in the summer, and soft and genial in the winter ... If proof were needed of the healthfulness of its inhabitants for generations past, one has only to examine the tombstones in the picturesque churchyard, on which the words 'Aged 80 years' appear with almost monotonous frequency." So it was written in the "Lymington Borough Guide" of 1920, extolling the virtues of the town.

Lymington churchyard contains many curious memorials, often obliterated during the course of time. One of the names recorded is that of John Northover, an old sea captain credited with having brought over the Czar, Peter the Great, from the land of the bears, when he paid a visit to William III in 1679. In May, 1735, Samuel Baldwyn of Lymington was immersed "sans ceremonie" off Scratchells Bay, south of the Needles, thereby encouraging his widow to carry out her vowed threat to dance on her husband's grave. Several tombs and headstones bear the names of foreign prisoners of war who died in Lymington during captivity. When the Civil War broke out in 1642, many tombstones were removed, probably for barricades. Prior to 1821, Lymington churchyard extended south of St. Thomas' Church, to what is now the centre of the High Street. This southern side was deemed a place of honour for interment, fit for the more worthy parishioners of the town.

In 1821 Sir Harry Burrard Neale presented the churchwardens with ¾-acre of fresh ground to the north part of Barfields for a churchyard extension, when the High Street was widened and the old churchyard cut back. Up until the mid-1800s, poor people were often buried without a coffin, and a bier to convey the corpse was retained at the parish expense. It was often the custom to bury nobility and more wealthy people at night, and in January, 1772, Miss Laura Burrard, a beautiful young heiress who died from a broken blood vessel at a society ball in Walhampton, was borne by night for burial at Lymington.

A proposal to build a church extension to St. Thomas' on part of the churchyard north of the church caused much controversy. The Ven. David Cartwright presided at a Consistory Court to hear parishioners' evidence before permission was granted for the removal of tombstones so that the new church hall could be added. This building was completed in 1981 at a cost of £176,180, offset by the sale of the Parish Hall in Emsworth Road for £194,000 to developers.

50 · Town Chest Safeguarded at Hurst Castle

Built as a fortress by Henry VIII in 1532 to guard against the French who had designs on invading the south of England, Hurst Castle protected the western entry to the Solent. Many of its original stones were taken from Beaulieu Abbey, and in 1574, as relations worsened with France, 100 men were stationed at the Castle. Following the outbreak of the Civil War in 1642, when Prince Rupert's ships were spotted in the Solent, Lymingtonians hurriedly arranged for the town's chest containing its records to be sent to Hurst Castle for safe keeping. When hostilities ceased in 1647, the Corporation made an entry: "for bringing the town chest from Hurst Castle, 2 shillings."

In November, 1647, Charles I escaped from Hampton Court to seek sanctuary with Col. Hammond at Carisbrooke Castle on the Isle of Wight. But there the King was arrested on December 1st and, accompanied by a retinue of some 15 servants, was shipped across the Solent to be held prisoner in a small room at Hurst Castle. For exercise, the royal captive took regular walks along the Hurst shingle spit. Around December 19th, the King was removed from Hurst and escorted to Windsor by a troop of horses which had been gathered in Lyndhurst.

Hurst Castle continued to serve as a prison with a permanent establishment of soldiers. In 1699 John Brent was taken there under warrant, for which the town of Lymington had to pay 4/-. Smuggling was rife along this coastline, and in 1699 the Chief Officer of the Customs House boat at Hurst was rewarded for detaining John Bath and his Lymington ship, the *Mary Ann*, with its cargo of linen, wine and other French goods from St. Malo. The lighthouses at Hurst and the Needles were constructed in 1786, and their lights were due to be finally examined from the sea on the night of September 29th; however, a storm prevented this, but the following night Capt. Bromfield managed to leave Lymington in the cutter *Rose*, and was able to report to Trinity House that the lights were "very bright".

During the reign of William III, an Act was passed preventing the spread of Catholicism, and in May, 1700, the Privy Council decreed Hurst Castle should act as a prison for such offenders, with sentence of "perpetual punishment". That year the Franciscan priest Father Paul Atkinson pleaded guilty at the Old Bailey to converting Elizabeth Rich to that faith. Despite many pleas on his behalf, the weakly monk was incarcerated at Hurst until his death there in 1729 at the age of 74.

During the First World War, when this photograph was taken, Hurst Castle became a prominent battlement, surrounded by barbed wire, with searchlights mounted in turrets to sweep the sea at night and complement the guns. And with the outbreak of the Second World War, the Castle was reoccupied by the Royal Artillery. It is now open to visitors as an historic monument.

Lymington Town station c., 1910.

The last steam train at Lymington Town station, April 2nd, 1967.

51 · First and Last Steam Trains

In 1844 Lymington Town Council passed a resolution pointing out the advantages of a railway communication with London and the west of England, in conjunction with "Castleman's Corkscrew" line – a twisting railway track through the Forest planned by Ringwood solicitor Charles Castleman, to link Brockenhurst with Ringwood and thence on to Wimborne and Dorchester. Nothing came of this Lymington resolution until, following the opening of the Southampton–Dorchester railway in 1847, and Brockenhurst station had been acquired by the London & South Western Railway Company, a public meeting was held in Lymington in August, 1853, when a motion was approved "to adopt measures for securing a branch railway from Brockenhurst to this town".

A local syndicate was formed, comprising banker George St. Barbe, Alfred Mew of Buckland Cottage, George Inman who owned the Lymington Shipyard, solicitors Richard Sharp and Edward Hicks, surgeon Charles Fluder, builder's merchant Philip Blake, Charles Estcourt, and William Squire of Yarmouth. The first two named were deputed to meet the Town Council on November 9th, 1855, seeking the councillors' support. The following March the mayor petitioned the House of Commons "for making a railway from Lymington, in the County of Southampton, to the London and South Western Railway, to be called the Lymington Railway, with a landing place at Lymington aforesaid, and for other purposes. That such a railway will in the opinion and judgment of this Council be very beneficial to the mercantile, shipping, and trading interest of this town; will afford great and much desired accommodation to the public generally, and especially in extension of the goods and passenger traffic between this town and the western parts of the Isle of Wight. Wherefore your Petitioners humbly pray that the said Bill may be passed into law."

The Act was duly passed in July, 1859, and the syndicate authorised to raise £21,000 capital by way of £10 shares. The Lymington Railway Company purchased the bridge between Lymington and Walhampton, with its powers to charge tolls on all who crossed, and the Quay from Lymington Corporation for the sum of £5,000. An Act was also approved authorising the Railway Company to acquire the halfpenny rowing-boat ferry which crossed the river from the Quay, but this was never taken up – instead it was sold by public auction to Mr. E.R. Badcock.

Construction of the four-mile railway track to Brockenhurst took 12 months, being completed in January, 1858. A temporary timber station near the Bridge Road railway crossing had to be used until the substantial brick station building was finally completed, on a former marshland site, once a saltern. So the official opening of the Lymington Railway Company's line took place on July 12th, 1858, to the accompaniment of the Town Band and church bells. In 1860 an unmanned halt was constructed at Shirley Holms, to cater for Sway and Boldre passengers, which remained in use for over forty years. The Company continued in operation until taken over by the London & South Western Railway on March 21st, 1879, who also acquired the rights of the toll bridge, which they leased to Mr. G. Gooden. In 1884 the railway track was extended southwards to the new Lymington Pier station, so that Isle of Wight ferries might perform at all states of the tide. The road toll bridge was subsequently passed into the ownership of the Southern Railway, and later acquired by Hampshire County Council, who eventually forfeited the toll rights in 1968. The last steam train (pictured) before electrification, left Lymington Town station on the night of April 2nd, 1967, with around 200 passengers crammed into the three carriages, and another 23 on the footplate despite the attempts of a railway inspector trying to keep control. The engine driver was Bert Farley, for whom this was also his last run, as he promptly retired after fifty years on the railway.

The imposing station now worthily merits Listed Building status.

December 1963, a branch line train prepares for a days' activity at Lymington Town.

Another M7 class crosses the river, headed for Brockenhurst.

52 · W.I. Members Sat at School Desks

This photograph shows members of Pennington Women's Institute taking part in Lymington Carnival during the mid-1930s. The banner on their float proclaims "Pennington's need for a Sports Field is urgent!", as the ladies seemed to think organisations were receiving priority use of the Lodge Road recreation ground, rather than the general public. Depicting the various sports were (left to right): Mrs. May Phillips, cyclist; Mrs. Dorothy Gale, footballer; Winnie Hall, hockey; Mrs. Namick, tennis; Mrs. Dolly Rickman, cricket; Mrs. Gwen Boyatt, netball; Mrs. Gladys Woodford, rounders; and Mrs. Lamb, bowls. These ladies valiantly stood on the float from its judging point in Avenue Road to Woodside, with Mrs. Phillips finding difficulty in holding her bicycle downhill, whilst Mrs. Gale was made to stand with one foot on a football along the entire route!

Pennington W.I. was founded in 1923, with just a dozen members above the qualifying age of 18. They held their evening meetings in Pennington School, sitting on the school pupils' forms, and the annual subscription was 2/6d. First president was Miss Helen Fullerton of Pennington Chase. In October, 1925, members formally opened their new £1,800 W.I. Hall off Ramley Road, in memory of the Institute's treasurer, Lady Nora Brand, who died the preceding year, wife of Rear-Admiral Sir Hubert Brand, of Yaldhurst. In 1926 Miss Fullerton waived a substantial part of her £400 loan to the Institute, and by this time membership had reached 114. Summer fetes were held at Ramley House, the drama and folk dancing groups won awards as far afield as Winchester and Bournemouth, and each year £10 was donated towards the village school's outing. Following Miss Fullerton's death in 1930, Mrs. Angela Brownlow of Pennington House succeeded as president.

In 1931, Pennington W.I. collected 2,033 eggs for Lymington Hospital, the largest amount contributed by any surrounding village – the eggs were preserved in "Glass's Fluid" for patients' consumption.

The hall letting charges were agreed at one guinea for an afternoon's wedding reception, two guineas for a dance, 30/- a concert. In 1932, Pennington joined three other institutes in the Borough demanding women magistrates be appointed on the Bench, forwarding a resolution to the Lord Chancellor. That same year Viscountess Frankfort was elected president. Along with members of Milford, Hordle and Everton Institutes, Pennington ladies performed "The Bride Feast" at the 1935 W.I. drama exhibition in London. Various improvements have been carried out to Pennington W.I. Hall: an £800 kitchen added in 1955, £900 toilets in 1971, a £15,000 roof in 1988. By that time membership numbered 110, and the Institute was still appearing in the annual Lymington Carnival procession.

53 · Memorial Tribute to Admiral

To the east of Lymington River, on Mount Pleasant, rises the 76' high granite obelisk erected to the memory of Admiral Sir Harry Burrard Neale, who entered the Royal Navy in early life, and went on to become a friend and shipmate of the King. The Burrard family owned the Walhampton Estate from 1688, and for almost two centuries members of that family served the town of Lymington as Mayor or Member of Parliament. The Admiral figured conspicuously in the war with republican France, managing to destroy twenty of the enemy's ships. One of his most notable achievements was to bring his ship, the *San Fiorenzo*, out of the Mutiny at the Nore in 1797, being the only officer to keep his crew under control. The drum which beat the officers and men to their quarters on that memorable occasion was presented to the Lymington Town Band's headquarters at the Literary Institute by a descendant, Francis Crozier. A sister of the Admiral, Harriet, was a great beauty and modelled for the artist Sir Joshua Reynolds.

In 1804 King George III, accompanied by the Queen and their Princesses, visited Sir Harry at Walhampton. His Majesty held a reception at Lymington town hall, and his attire greatly impressed the locals as he paraded in the High Street in a green coat with gold buttons, buckskins and a cocked hat. Mr. Tout, the Sergeant-at-Mace, dressed in his insignia of office, was so overcome that he dropped on his knees before the King, exclaiming: "I am like a beast before thee."

Such was the high esteem in which the Admiral was held by the townsfolk of Lymington that, upon his death in 1840, the obelisk was erected in his memory for a sum of £1,482 3s., mostly from public subscription. In recognition of these donations, the family executed a deed allowing the public free access to the memorial site. Victorian coins were placed under a corner stone.

By 1892 Francis Crozier, who had acquired the freehold of the site, presented the landmark to the Lymington Corporation, along with a £100 gift in order that a fund be set up to ensure it was maintained in good condition. Mr. Crozier had married Sir George Burrard's elder daughter Harriet, was a Judge in India, and lived for forty years at Delawarr House, Woodside, Lymington. On the death of his wife in 1877, such was his grief that he built a Sunday School at Woodside in her memory.

Inscriptions on the four faces of the obelisk tell of the Admiral's courage and zeal, also recording his representation of Lymington in many Parliaments over forty years: "His anxious desire was ever to do good and to promote the prosperity of his native town". The obelisk site continues to remain the responsibility of Lymington Town Council, though it lies in the parish of Boldre.

The Obelisk, Lymington

54 · Four Generations of Undertakers

A view looking towards the western end of St. Thomas' Street, festooned in bunting at the time of the Coronation of King Edward VII in 1902. Standing outside his Nos. 33 and 34 shop fronts, on the far right, is Mr. Frederick William House, the upholsterer and undertaker. He had previously served 15 years as manager of Mr. E.R. Badcock's furnisher's workshop in the High Street, before deciding to set up on his own in 1898 – when Mr. Badcock forecast Fred would be back in his employ within six months. Despite such discouragement, Fred acquired the two shops, the one on the left having been Mr. E.J. Cox's leather goods shop, and the other occupied by Mr. H.E. Prince the cabinet maker and confectioner. Fred made a success of his own venture, which included making window blinds, beating and relaying carpets, and making all kinds of bedding and loose-covers. He often cut linoleum on the pavement outside the shop, and young grandson Ronald received 2d. for the Sunday morning chore of polishing customers' cutlery – in days before stainless steel blades – by cranking the handle of an 1870 Kent's Knife Cleaner machine, in which polishing powder was inserted. Fred is photographed with his daughter Ellen, who later married Henry Bale, a corporal in the Somerset Light Infantry. When Fred finally retired in 1935, he handed the business over to his son Charles Edward. He in turn retired more than a quarter of a century later to live on Stanford Hill, when grandson Ron took control, then Nigel House became the fourth generation in charge.

Pictured next door is the imposing house Wistaria, the private residence of Mr. John King, who ran a large corn and seed merchant's store from Nos. 20-22, St. Thomas' Street, on the opposite side of the road. The dark-fronted property next to Wistaria, 31, St. Thomas' Street, was known as Old Town Meeting, the Presbyterian (later Independent) chapel, for more than a century before the wor-

shippers built their new Congregational (now United Reformed) Church in the High Street in 1847, along with its own day-school and parsonage, for the sum of £4,500. The last service to be held in the Old Town Chapel was held on October 24th, 1847. In the little house next door, Mr. Charles Percy Jones rented the front room for his solicitor's business. Next comes the shop front of No. 28, where Mr. Ben Winsey and son Ben jnr. ran a boot and shoe repairing business from 1911-76. This is followed by the large frontage of Keeping's Garage and coachbuilding works, part of which was demolished for the Co-operative Wholesale Society to build their grocery and butchery store, which lay much further back from the pavement kerb as the planners had intended to widen the roadway. Next to the Garage, Mr. Bert Cox ran his high-class confectionery shop. Then followed the two shops of Mr. "Windy" Westwood, the first a grocer's, and the next ironmongery and hardware. On the corner with Queen Street was the Corner 'Paper Shop. Facing down the street can be seen Miller's butcher's shop and Hawkins' Dairy – both long since pulled down to convert the narrow Priestlands Place (once known as Soapy Lane) into the main road one-way system around the top of the town.

LYMINGTON. St. Thomas' Street. Coronation Decorations.

55 · The Last Picture Show

At a meeting of the directors of the Lymington & New Forest Entertainments Ltd., held at their registered office in 38, High Street, on Thursday, July 24th, 1913, the following tenders were received for the building of a cinema: F.J. Pearce, £2,370; Stone & St. John, £2,296; Sam Elgar & Son, £2,185; Rashley & Co. £2,185; and W. Hackwell, £2,165. These were all considered too high, so architect Mr. Benjamin was ordered to make modifications so as to reduce the price to £1,800, with the last three mentioned firms asked to submit new tenders. Eventually Rashley's figure of £1,768 10s., less 2½% for surveyor's fees, was accepted. It was later agreed to add a further £25 for a brick frontage instead of cement. It was resolved that the seating comprise ten rows at 3d. a ticket, six at 6d. three at 1/-, and three at 1/6d. A Werhner piano was acquired for £30, and Mr. Badcock carpeted the whole hall for £64. Mr. Dibley was appointed film operator at £1 10s. a week, Miss Pelfrey cashier for 8/- a week, and there were many applicants for the posts of doorkeeper and chocolate sales girls.

So the Lyric Cinema opened for entertainment in December, 1913, but the County Architect closed the premises the following February for further roof strengthening work, so all the staff were laid off with one week's notice in lieu of wages, whilst Mr. Elgar, the manager, was dismissed for his conduct with young girls in the cinema, lack of smartness, and allowing encores when the doors should be open to admit the second house. When the Lyric reopened, Mr. Wincote was appointed the new manager at £2 a week. The directors took out a £1,250 mortgage with the Capital & Counties Bank. The cinema also staged local entertainment by such organisations as the Lymington Philharmonic Society, but with so many young men called up for First World War Service, the Lyric incurred a £226 18s. 11d. loss during its first year.

In September, 1919, it was agreed to introduce Sunday evening performances, despite condemnation from the pulpit by the Vicar. At the eighth annual meeting in 1921 chairman Mr. G. Vicary commented "The fickle public found a new toy for the winter months in the People's Theatre, and for a time the Lyric was in the background." The People's Theatre had originated in a marquee off Grove Road, before transferring to the Literary Institute – however, they also went through a bad spell, and its proprietor Mr. Hayes left some months before the expiration of his lease. By 1922 the average weekly hire of films at the Lyric was £11 16s., and manager Mr. B. Wincote received a £10 bonus in appreciation of his efforts, with the year's total receipts £2,972 and trading expenses of £2,397.

An alteration in the Finance Act of 1924 led to the admission charge for the first section of seats being reduced to 1/3d., with the second section 8d. and the third 5d. In 1930 Mr. Wincote was surprised to receive one week's notice, and Mr. Walter Mouland was appointed the new manager. He was also the fire station officer, before he collapsed and died in his cinema office in 1961, and the Lyric closed two years later with the popularity of television. This photograph shows the cinema as it was in July, 1963.

The last film to be shown was *Mrs. Gibbons Boys* starring Diana Dors and Lionel Jeffries on 1st June, 1963.

56 · Favourite Haunt for Smugglers

The Woodside village area of Lymington forms a very old, and sometimes notorious, part of the town. The *Fisherman's Rest* pub was called Grattens Cottage before Mr. James Bran was granted the first liquor licence in 1870, when it became a favourite haunt for local smugglers. Just discernable in this photograph, taken around 1910, is Ted Salter, standing with his bicycle between the two young lasses. Ted, who lived in the house on the right, was a self-employed painter and decorator, and became the envy of the entire neighbourhood when he acquired his new Raleigh bicycle. Such was his delight in owning this fine machine that he rode it for the considerable distance to London and back, despite the discomfort of solid wheels on gravel roads.

In the house next door to Ted lived Mr. Percy Bennett with his wife Alice and their eight children; Percy daily walked to and from his employment at Sway Timberworks. In the middle cottage lived Lot Broomfield, a decorator, with his wife Nellie and their family of twelve children. The end property was occupied by Jake Hayter, who made boots and shoes for the local gentry, using wooden pegs and no nails. Jake was a cripple, who had to walk with crutches when not riding in his trap-cart hauled by a donkey.

57 · Mr. Bartlett's Popular Amusement Fair

One familiar face around Lymington early this century was that of Mr. Bill Gates the bill poster, who lived in Stanford Road. He could be seen cycling around the town with a bucket of adhesive paste hanging from his handlebars, a long-handled brush strapped to the crossbar, with a large bag full of posters hung over his shoulder. These posters advertised local happenings, such as dances, auctions or household sales. Of particular interest were the 20" x 15" yellow posters Mr. Gates erected around Lymington every May and October, eagerly awaited by young and old, heralding the impending visit of Bartlett's Fun Fair in the Gas Works Field, Gosport Street – now the Fairlea Road housing estate. Shopkeepers willing to display such posters in their windows were rewarded with free rides at the Fair.

Pictured right is Mr. Bartlett's popular *New Forest Hunters* galloping horses roundabout, on which hundreds of Lymington adults and children derived great enjoyment. It was Mr. James Bartlett who established the Fair in 1840 from Home Farm, Blissford, near Fordingbridge. Originally the horse-drawn train of waggons – little more than improvised farm waggons – were used to pull their fairground loads and box-type living vans with iron-tyred wheels. They travelled widely through Hampshire, Dorset and Wiltshire. A considerable transformation came in 1889, when the centre truck of the by now steam-operated "set of galloping horses" weighing 4½ tons was hauled by a farm traction engine instead of the customary team of horses. In 1890 Bartlett's acquired the second showman's engine built by Burrell's, named *Queen of the South*, then in 1896 they purchased yet another Burrell, *Majestic*.

Three or four loads of coloured waggons and living vans were drawn by traction and showman steam engines, painted maroon and yellow with red linings, the largest weighing over 17 tons. Lymington was always the first and last stopping site each season. These huge loads would chug their way across the New Forest, stopping only at streams to draw up additional water for thirsty boilers. Mr. Bartlett – a true showman – insisted his entourage came to a halt near Buckland Manor House on the Southampton Road entrance to Lymington, so that his machinery be given an extra polish before entering the town. These engines would trundle along Queen Street and St. Thomas' Street, turn right down Church Lane and into The Grove, then left along South Street (since renamed Captain's Row) and finally into Gosport Street. A feather of steam might perhaps emit from an engine's polished brass tubes – but Mr. Bartlett considered a driver inefficient if the safety valves continuously blew off steam.

Turning into Union Hill (now East Hill), the leading driver would apply wooden brake blocks behind his rear wheels to prevent his waggons rolling backwards whilst waiting for Frank, son of Harry Golding, to unlock the five-barred gate to the Gas Works Field. With merely inches to spare, each waggon and trailer would squeeze through this narrow entrance. The other photograph, taken around 1919, shows Mr. Bartlett's 1892, 8 n.h.p. two-speed single-cylinder Burrell traction engine *Queen of the South*, works number 1642, which was later sold to the Chipperfield family of circus fame.

Lymington youngsters clamoured to ride on the *New Forest Hunters*, or stand in wonderment gazing at the figures in the glass-cased organ – the bandmaster, bell and triangle player, the snare and bass drummers – accompanying the music, which was originally barrel-type, later altered to book-type. This book-operated organ was driven from an engine mounted on the front of the Tidman Centre Engine, which rotated the roundabouts. A belt from the flywheel of the organ engine engaged another, to operate double cranks, from which levers connected to a pair of bellows beneath the organ. These produced the air for the trumpets, organ pipes, and movement of the figures.

Bartlett's visited the Lymington showground each May and October from the late nineteenth century until the outbreak of the Second World War in 1939, by which time it was run by Mrs. Polly Bartlett, the second wife of Alfred, son of James.

Rides on the *New Forest Hunters* cost ½d. for children and 1d. for adults – other amusements included coconut shies, 3 balls for 1d.; swinging boats 1d. for adults only; darts 3 for 1d. Mrs. Gertie Manley, a member of the troupe, had queues of customers for her home-made toffee apples and brandy snaps. The Bartlett family had a long-standing arrangement with the owner of the Gas Works Field, Harry ("Farmer Fatty") Golding, who weighed over twenty stone. He lived in the bungalow Maycross, which still stands on East Hill, and from there he sold milk, butter and cheese provided by the cows in his fields opposite and below the bungalow.

J. Bartlett's 'gallopers', The New Forest Hunters c., 1900.

Queen of the South c., 1919.

58 · Four Famous Pubs

A photograph of the High Street around 1920, when the earliest motor vehicles were to be seen in the town. The impressive timbered building on the extreme right is the *Anchor & Hope* Hotel, which dates back to 1747 and was originally known as *The Crown*. In coaching days, the Telegraph coach left from this hotel each day at 5 a.m., and another at 5.45 p.m.; the journey to Southampton took 2½ hours, and London 11 hours. The Bud of Hope Lodge of the Manchester Union of Oddfellows was founded in 1845, using this hotel as their headquarters for regular meetings. In 1905 the *Anchor & Hope* was destroyed by fire, and the Lodge's records incinerated. The fire was one of the worst Lymington had known, with bystanders fearful that the entire town would burn down. In modern times this hotel has suffered the fate of many in the High Street, acquired by an estate agent and building society.

Two street traders are pictured offering their goods outside the *Anchor & Hope*, the nearest being Jim Young's wet-fish cart, the other being protected by a handsome awning. Oysters and other shellfish, along with fruit and vegetables, were sold at the kerbside by such traders.

The shop premises beyond the *Anchor & Hope* was the tailoring business of Alderman Edward Stone, one of Lymington's longest serving mayors, before the premises was acquired by Mr. W. Stephens, and later Mr. R.C. Moore the fruiterer, eventually becoming Bateman's the opticians; next door, in No. 94, was Thomas Gray the saddler; No. 93 was occupied by Mr. W. Green the pork butcher until, just before the Second World War, the shop was sold to the London Central Meat Co., and later to Baxter's who enlarged the premises by converting 93 and 94 into one shop. Next, on the corner of New Street, came Mr. E.R. Badcock, the estate agent, a sedate man who strode across the High Street to his drapery shop on the opposite side of the road insisting that motorised traffic should give him right of way. On the left-hand side of the picture, at the corner of Ashley Lane, can be seen the drapery business of William Boothby Rand, who opened at 7, St. Thomas' Street in 1876, before moving with son Herbert to 43, High Street, in 1910, where they stocked the largest range of fabrics anywhere along the south coast.

The *Red Lion* pub with the long flagpole on the right dates from around the 1600s. Next shop along, 112, High Street, was the ironmonger's business founded by George Hapgood in 1848, and continued by succeeding generations of that family until 1981. Nos. 110 and 111 was the drapers' and clothiers' shop which George Bennett & Sons ran for almost a century. Children would watch with fascination as counter staff placed customers' cash inside a metal cylinder, which was screwed into an overhead cable; a spring-loaded trigger sent the cylinder flying along to the cashier's desk at the other end of the shop, where a receipt and any change were inserted back in the cylinder before it was sent back by cable to the original counter. The shop was later purchased by Tesco.

George Meane was the proprietor of the *Londesborough Hotel*, at 34, High Street, previously known as the Nag's Head Inn. He advertised its well-stocked cellars, fine old wines and spirits, and cigars of the finest quality. There were posting and livery stables to the rear, along with extensive greenhouses and gardens to provide produce for its excellent cuisine. These grounds were later occupied by the Hants & Dorset Bus Company depot. Seen below is Mr. Backhurst when he progressed from horse-drawn carriage drives to motorised taxis, which he and his sons operated from the mews at the rear of the *Angel Hotel* for many years (below).

Anchor & Hope, High St. c., 1920.

The Londesborough Hotel, 34 High St.

The Red Lion c., 1910.

59 · Early Motoring

The arrival of the motorised vehicle in Lymington brought a mixed reception, for many objected to its speed, noise and the stench from exhaust fumes. This picture right shows one of the first motor accidents in the town, on the corner of Nelson Place with Captain's Row, when a Thornycroft lorry from the Wessex Oil & Petrol Co. of Quay Road, managed by Mr. W.E. Carson, knocked over Brights' delivery lorry from Bournemouth. Nevertheless, the motor car and motor cycle afforded greater travel opportunities, as depicted with their occupants skating on the thick ice at Hatchett Pond, Beaulieu, in 1933.

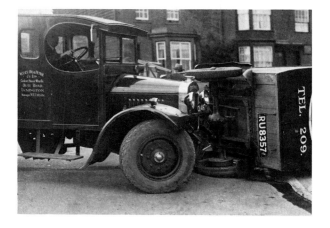

60 · Wayside Refreshment

Drivers of horse-drawn vehicles found their animals often needed to conveniently stop at inns around the town to rest awhile. Right is the *Hare & Hounds* at Sway in the early 1920s, with licensees Mr. and Mrs. Bacon (nee Hobby) standing at the entrance with their daughter Ivy. Below is the *Crown* at Everton, where Mr. and Mrs. Underwood were the licensees during the First World War, when they formed close friendships with many of the Indian soldiers stationed at Milford. Their daughter Dorothy Underwood was a talented singer with the Lymington Philharmonic Society, who performed at the Lyric Cinema and other venues around the town.

61 · John Howlett, Engineer Extraordinary

One man who did probably more than any other single person to bring prosperity to the town was John Howlett. He started work as a 14 year old boy with the famous steam engine manufacturers Charles Burrell & Sons in Thetford, Norfolk, where his father was also employed as a carpenter. Young John, a 4/- a week apprentice, sought to improve his learning by attending evening classes. He went on to become a chargehand with the Daimler motor company at Coventry, and his quest for greater engineering knowledge took him on to the Wolseley repair depot in London, where he once worked on Queen Alexandra's car, and later to the Austin car company.

Then John was recommended to Mr. Hamilton Dent as a prospective manager for South Coast Garages at Lymington. Relishing the opportunity to work for himself, he arrived in 1912, when the population of the town was just over 4,000, and yacht building was the only principal industry. South Coast Garages owed £4,000 at that time, and John took the risk of investing his own personal savings. Nevertheless he gradually built up a flourishing repair trade on their Stanford Road site — but with the onset of the First World War, almost all of his nine mechanics left to fight for their country, and by 1916 South Coast Garages seemed destined for bankruptcy.

But John, in conjunction with his close friend Mr. St. George Caulfield, who owned a machine shop at nearby Vicar's Hill, Boldre, managed to obtain a contract to manufacture one hundred 18 lb. shells, which the Army found in short supply. This in turn led to a regular contract for 500 shells a week, so more employees, including local women, were engaged on the workforce. John's success as a determined salesman resulted in an agreement for South Coast Garages to supply the Air Ministry with 10,000 piston rings at 1/9d. a piece for Gnome Monosoupape engines — and this later led to further piston ring orders for the Bentley rotary aero engine, and for A.E.C. omnibus engines.

Finding the name South Coast Garages something

of a drawback, in 1919 the new title of Wellworthy Ltd. was established as a private company. The shareholders were John Howlett, William Gray, J.B. Perkins and C.E. Jones, the latter pair having provided most of the finance — but with poor prospects in the post-war period, both later decided to withdraw, and Mr. Howlett bought up their shares with borrowed money. High costs led to Wellworthy incurring a £950 loss over the next 18 months — but then came their first major order, supplying the Armstrong-Siddeley company with 20,000 piston rings at 5½d. each, thereby undercutting the British Piston Ring Co. by ½d. per ring. In 1921 the Wellworthy workforce numbered just over 30, and the machinery was housed in a 120' x 100' factory at Stanford Road. In 1922 the company took a trade stand at the first Motor Show in Olympia, and that year £302 was spent on advertising, representing 1.6% of total sales.

Mr. Howlett insisted on a thorough inspection of every ring, and whilst watching the Schneider Cup air race trials over the Solent, noticed blue smoke emitting from the exhaust of the British entry, indicating heavy oil consumption; this led to the Rolls-Royce engines being fitted with Wellworthy rings which proved an instant cure, and ultimately resulted in the great success of the wartime Spitfire fighter. Backed by an energetic team of directors, Wellworthy expanded with the opening of a second large site in Lymington, at Ampress, in 1939. The firm worked round the clock during the Second World War, and other factories followed at Ringwood, Salisbury, Weymouth, Waterford in Ireland, and Plymouth. By 1969 sales reached £10-million, and six years later Wellworthy employed 1,800 people in Lymington alone. Mr. Howlett died in 1977, having been succeeded as managing director by Arthur Woolcott.

Wellworthy became part of the Associated Engineering Group, and were pioneers in the squeeze-casting technique, with exports as far distant as China and the United States. A recession in the 'eighties led to the sale of the original Stanford Road site for a supermarket and, following a merger with one-time manufacturing arch-rivals Hepworth & Grandage, Wellworthy finally severed all its roots with Lymington in 1989. By then only a mere handful of local workers remained, and they were dispersed to the other factories.

Stanford Road frontage in the 1920s.

Some of the staff towards end of First World War. John Howlett on the left.

The Radial works, Stanford Road in the early 30s.

Wellworthy's in the 1950s.

62 · Rashley & Co's Building Works

Pictured on the extreme right is the premises of Rashley's the builders. William Banks operated such a business at this site from 1834 or earlier, and in those days young apprentices signed indentures forbidding any contract into matrimony, playing cards or dice, or haunting taverns or playhouses, during their five-year apprenticeship. J. Rashley and J. Springer took over the High Street premises in 1859, and many prestigious contracts were won, such as building the palatial Victoria Hotel on Milford clifftop in 1890. The firm was known as the South Hants Building Works until 1905, when Tom Rashley formed a partnership with Frank Totterdell, Richard Bower, and his son Percy Rashley. By 1906 their labourers were paid 7d. an hour, scaffolders 7½d., painters 10d., bricklayers and carpenters 10½d., plasterers and plumbers 11d. Tom retired in 1911 to White Cottage, a house he built in Milford, but he died a few years later.

Rashley's continued to prosper, with over 110 employees on their payroll. The firm repaired the sea wall in 1913, and properties built included the Lyric Cinema in 1913, the Chewton Glen Hotel at New Milton in 1914, the Parish Hall off Emsworth Road in 1924, and the Througham Place mansion near Beaulieu in 1926 (burned down in 1979), also the new sacristy at St. Thomas' Church in 1931, and Dawson's Garage, next door to Rashley's own High Street premises, in 1938.

Frank Totterdell died in 1938, Percy Rashley the following year, and former churchwarden Richard Bower in 1942. The last active member of those families, Richard's son Ted Bower, retired in 1954. Subsequent directors were Mike Matthews (who joined Rashley's in 1946), Gordon Burgess (1951), and Arthur Trigell (1955). In 1984 the company celebrated 125 years' service to the town.

Pictured next beyond Rashley's is The Invincible Motor Works, at 76, High Street, run by Mr. G.T. Vince, who also operated a taxi business from his vehicle repair workshop to the rear of the site. These premises were later occupied by South Coast Garages, before being taken over by Dawson Bros. in 1931, who had previously run their business from 10, St. Thomas' Street. In 1990 No. 76 became a shopping parade, Lymington Antiques Centre.

HIGH STREET & CHURCH, LYMINGTON.

63 · Pilley Congregational Chapel

At one time parishioners of Boldre were considered a most turbulent and uncivilised fraternity. When William Gilpin, headmaster of Cheam School for 25 years, arrived at Boldre as Vicar in 1777, he wrote that the people of Boldre "are little better than a set of bandits". He caused a great improvement in their morals, and proved a remarkable reformer by building a Poor House and a model school, which still bears his name.

In 1810 the Rev. John Davies, a young preacher from Gosport Academy, became minister at Lymington Congregational Church and realised the need to evangelise the New Forest villages of nearby Pilley and East End. The Rev. Richard Adams became village pastor, and although he possessed no pretensions to scholarship, was "a walking library" concerning history and theology, and "would sometimes carry his audience to the very gate of heaven, and at others he would try the patience of all his hearers by dullness and prolixity." The Congregationalists, or Independents as they were known in those days, extended their evangelism to Hurst Castle.

At Pilley they met in one anothers' houses as a mission station until, in 1857, a triangular piece of Forest land was purchased by Mr. Robert Stroud so that the Dissenting Christians might have a regular place of worship. The money was raised within a year of the opening of this chapel in 1858. In 1913 the Pilley chapel was granted the status of a branch church, able to administer their own affairs and hold their own meetings; should membership fall below 20 they would revert to a mission station. Such was the poverty of the Pilley members that the chapel had its own Women's Slate Club, a Coal Club, a Clothing Club, and a Men's Slate Club. A new Sunday School room was added in 1926 at a cost of £330. Numbers had increased to 62 by 1939, when electricity was installed in the building. For the centenary in 1958, the congregation overflowed into the schoolroom, where the service was relayed by loudspeaker. In 1981 the chapel suffered severely from internal dissension, and despite the intervention of the provincial moderator, many members and their children withdrew. The chapel finally closed eight years later, with the deacons' intention that the building be converted into housing.

64 · The Six Bells

The town band and hundreds of Lymingtonians crowded the High Street when the new octave of church bells for St. Thomas' arrived by horse and cart in 1901. The Vicar, Canon Maturin, is seen centre foreground. The heaviest bell, the tenor, weighing over a ton, was carried on the cart of Bill Phillips, pictured with arm on hips in the centre. After the bells were hung on a new steel frame, the bell-ringers, trained by Mr. George Preston of Christchurch, rang a quarter-peal in 1904, and a three-hour peal in 1906. These feats were duly recorded on engraved stone tablets in the bell tower.

The *Six Bells* pub, next to the *Dorset Arms*, was named after the six bells in St. Thomas' Church tower, and acted as the headquarters for the thirsty bellringers after practice sessions. On July 7th, 1814, this inn provided beer for the peace celebrations. It eventually closed on December 28th, 1911, and later became Aldridge's Dairy, run by Mr. Trowbridge.

ARRIVAL OF CHURCH BELLS AT LYMINGTON 1901

65 · From Garage to Newsagent's

Dawson's Garage occu-
pied No. 10 St. Tho-
mas' Street, where the
1928 6-cylinder Lea Francis car
seen in the showroom was offered "tax paid to end of year,
only done 250 miles, £475 or
near offer". Dawson's moved to
76, High Street, in 1931.

No. 11, St. Thomas' Street,
was the newsagent's shop of
mayor Alderman Gibson. When
he retired in 1933, Fred Totterdell, who had worked at King's
since 1888, joined son Fred jnr.,
a solicitor's clerk with Heppen-
stalls, and daughter-in-law Lily,
who ran a toy and sweet shop
opposite at No. 31, to jointly
take over the newsagency. In
1940 grandson John joined the
family business, which moved to
No. 10 next door in 1967. It was
sold to N.S.S. in 1973, later
Forbuoys.

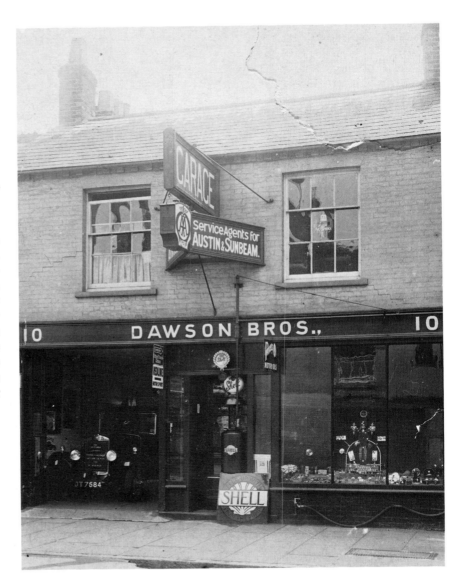

66 · Destroyed by an Incendiary Bomb

St. Thomas' Church was served by ministers until 1869, when the Rev. Benjamin Maturin succeeded in his claim to the status of Vicar. He was the incumbent at Lymington for over half-a-century, from 1852-1905, becoming Rural Dean and an Honorary Canon of Winchester Cathedral. This photograph shows the large turnout of parishioners watching the coffin being lifted from Mr. Badcock's horse-drawn hearse at the Canon's funeral on November 4th, 1905.

Pictured at the rear is the furniture broker's shop of Charles Ford. He came from Southampton to open 47-48, St. Thomas' Street in 1840, and lived over the shop with his wife Emma. They sold furniture, china, glass, and carpets, and daughter Sarah later joined the business. She married Alfred Isted, who duly became a partner with Charles Ford. They added furniture removals to their enterprise, using vehicles drawn by horses which were stabled in Church Lane, with grazing in the nearby field which later became the site of the Lyric Cinema car park. Charles Ford died in 1902, and Alfred Isted the following year. Sarah continued to run the firm, assisted by sons Charles and Alfred and daughter Vera.

In 1905 additional premises were acquired on the opposite side of the road, 61 and 62, High Street, previously Lamble's the grocers. The ladies took charge of running the Ford's business when the men were conscripted for First World War service. Soon after these hostilities, Ford's delivery transport became mechanised with the purchase of a huge Leyland lorry with open driver's cab, which also hauled a large trailer. A large brick warehouse was built in Western Road. In 1928 the St. Thomas' Street premises were modernised with a new shopfront – only to be destroyed by an incendiary bomb in 1941. Eight members of the two Isted families had been called up for Second World War service, two of whom were killed. The St. Thomas' Street shop was eventually rebuilt in 1961. The year 1990 marked the 150th anniversary of the firm, when members of the Isted families still serving were Geoff, Alan, Ken and Patricia.

The handsome street lamp seen by the church – later resited by the Yacht Club – was provided by public subscription in 1832 as a tribute to Admiral Sir Harry Neale, for providing all the iron columns for street lamps in the town, and to George Burrard, for donating the lamps on top of the columns.

Funeral of the Late Rev: Canon Maturin. Nov: 4. 1905.

67 · Newlands Manor

In 1793 Sir John D'Oyley resided at Newlands Manor, Everton, when he sold the house and estate to Admiral the Hon. Sir William Cornwallis, close friend of Napoleon. Much of the property was burned down through the carelessness of a servant on Christmas Day, 1801. A fireplace had been over-stoked, causing excessive heat. It happened to be a Sunday, and the congregation at All Saints' Church could see the glow of the flames through the church windows. The Vicar was at a loss to understand why worshippers were gradually leaving their pews during the middle of his sermon. They had gone to give assistance – but all to no avail, as the Newlands building was so badly damaged that it had to be rebuilt. The pinnacled structure was finally completed in 1805.

The impressive manor house was the scene of many fine, fashionable balls, and frequent visitors included King Edward VII, who struck up an intimate relationship with Mrs. Cornwallis-West. Her son George married Lady Randolph Churchill, who was twenty years his senior – and the betrothal greatly displeased her son Winston Churchill, for he was sixteen days older than his new step-father. This marriage ended thirteen years later, when George married the beautiful actress, Mrs. Patrick Campbell. She revelled in her new, more sedate,

lifestyle, going on to record "the deep bliss of the double bed after the hurly-burly of the chaise-longue". In 1920 the Newlands Manor Estate passed on to Sir John Power, but when his health failed in 1948, the manor house was divided into eleven residential apartments.

Seen above is the steam traction engine used by Mr. Hubert Gale snr. in the 1930s to drive the machinery at his Flanders Farm, Hordle.

68 · The Bridge at Boldre

Boldre Bridge, when the highway was a dirt road. On the opposite side of the river, the house on the right side of the road is Boldre Bridge Cottage, built in 1786. It was once occupied by butcher George Lewis (born 1795) who, with his wife Mary, had previously been the master and mistress of Boldre's new workhouse opened by the Vicar, the Rev. William Gilpin, in 1793 on the site of the present William Gilpin School, with about 35 inhabitants, whose ages ranged from three to 84. Boldre Bridge Cottage was later owned by the Wellstead family, carriers and coal merchants, who also baked bread in the kitchen which they sold through the large front window.

Seen right is Heywood Mill House, Boldre, further upriver, built in 1750 or later, and extended in 1812 by Jenvey the joiner, who was also the parish clerk.

Boldre Bridge.

Heywood Mill House, Boldre.

69 · Town Hill and Quay Hill

The foot of the town hill. No. 1, High Street, was occupied by William Moger, who sold antique furniture, whilst the Balls family ran Nos. 2-5 for their radio business, and sold prams on the opposite side of the road. The white-tiled shop on the left was the British & Colonial Meat Co. shop.

Also pictured is Belmore Lane, Lymington, with the *Millwrights' Arms* on the right, where the last licence was issued on February 15th, 1915. This photograph was taken before the thatched cottages beyond were badly damaged in "The Great Fire of Lymington" on May 27th, 1913. They were owned by Mr. "Postman" Brown.

Quay Hill in 1930, with the *Solent Inn* at the foot, constructed originally as a gentleman's residence in 1700 with a bowling green to the rear. On the bottom right of the hill was *The Alarm Inn*, named after Mr. Weld's famous yacht, and on the extreme right is the *King's Head*, where the landlord in 1836 was Thomas Avery. The bottom left-hand house was occupied by Mr. Winkworth, who traded in rabbit skins.

Top: Town Hill.
Middle: Belmore Lane.
Bottom: Quay Hill.

70 · The Hall Family's Greengrocery Shop

No. 122, High Street, pictured in 1932, when Frederick James Hall and his wife Victoria Maude acquired the premises from Mr. Gauntlett, a bookmaker. Fred was serving in the Army Medical Corps during the First World War when he married Miss Victoria Harrison, who was born at Quay Hill. Whilst on active service in France, Fred suffered a burst varicose vein and had to crawl his way to reach a hospital for life-saving treatment.

When he and Victoria took over 122, High Street, they sold fruit, vegetables, flowers, eggs, cigarettes and confectionery from the shop. Many of the vegetables they grew themselves in the large garden at the rear of the shop, which stretched back as far as the old Police Station in Gosport Street, with tomatoes grown around the perimeter walls. Victoria also catered for Cycling Tourist Union members during the summer, with meals eaten on the premises, and she also ran a registry office for servants, charging half-a-crown when a vacancy was filled. There was also a "You May Phone from Here" public telephone in the shop: Lymington 231.

Victoria also managed to give birth to five children, two of whom died in infancy. The sole remaining son, Jack Harrison Hall, helped deliver goods by trade bicycle over a radius of five

miles, and collected eggs from a farm near Sway. As a 14 year old Lymington Sea Scout, young Jack was privileged to be included in a party escorted by Scout leader Robert Hole to the Scouts' world jamboree in Holland, in 1937. Jack's mother died suddenly of cerebral haemorrhage in 1937 at the age of 49, and her heartbroken husband also died a few weeks later. On either side of the shop at this time was Blachford's hairdressers at No. 121, and Figgures' china shop in 123. Mr. Figgures afterwards bought No. 122 for his electrical shop.

71 · A Pennington Farm

The Orman family owned the large tract of farmland on the eastern side of Ramley Road, Pennington. They grew vegetables on the site of the present Pennington Junior School, which they sold in their village shop, and kept a herd of 92 T.T. attested Guernsey cows on the remainder of the land, which stretched north to the cemetery. A gravel path with a kissing-gate ran across their land from Pennington Square towards Highfield. Joseph Orman handed the farm over to his son and daughter-in-law Harold and Ivy in 1945, and they fought the Borough Council's compulsory purchase order to acquire part of the farmland to extend the cemetery. The Ormans lost the day, had to pay £200 legal fees, and were forced to sell the cattle as they would now have to cross a road — strictly forbidden for a T.T. herd. So Harold switched to pig farming. The farm was eventually sold in 1957, which led to the start of the Priestlands Road housing development.

The aerial picture of 1922 shows Pennington as a tightly knit community around the village square. It was not until after the Second World War that there was a great influx of new inhabitants. At the time of the photograph, the churchyard had just been extended to accommodate new graves.

The Orman's village shop.

Pennington 1922.

72 · Cannon from the Crimea

On May 29th, 1856, a festival was arranged in Lymington so that its inhabitants might celebrate the welcome news of peace with Russia. The event provoked much gaiety, and one spectacular tableau devised to commemorate this memorable occasion was a gas "star", considered by townsfolk to be a great novelty. However, this proved something of an anti-climax, for the "star" did not prove a success, owing to the gas pipe being too small in diameter.

Nevertheless, on January 25th, 1858, the mayor, John Hayward, in a moment of patriotic fervour, felt obliged to make an application to Lord Panmure, asking that one of the Russian cannons captured during the Crimean war be presented to Lymington as a gift to the town. The mayor's request received approval, and a subscription was made to defray the cost of an iron carriage on which to mount the gun.

The town complied with a War Office suggestion that the carriage be made at the royal arsenal at Woolwich, London.

So the impressive large gun duly arrived in Lymington, to be situated in the centre of the road at the northern end of New Street, near the Infirmary. The cannon proved a popular plaything for local children, who would clamber up the gun carriage and slide their way along the long barrel – sometimes incurring the wrath of parents when tearing their clothing. The cannon remained on this site for around a century, until it was removed during the Second World War and melted down for armaments. The narrow highway leading off New Street, opposite its junction with Emsworth Road, was named Cannon Lane, later changed to Cannon Street – and indeed New Street was at one time known as New Lane.

THE CANNON
LYMINGTON

73 · When a Morning Coat Cost £4 10s.

Mr. John Jenvey operated his tailor's business in Queen Street before moving to 9, St. Thomas' Street, in 1909, and he worked there until his eighties before sons George and Ernest took over in 1929 – George ran the business side, whilst Ernest acted as workshop foreman, after both had received a good grounding in the trade. In 1912 there was a staff of ten men on the premises, plus two male and two female outside workers. Their clientele included prominent ladies and gentlemen from the surrounding area – and indeed could claim royal patronage when the Princess Royal paid a call whilst she was passing through Lymington. Only the best cloth was used, with a wide selection from which to choose, and in 1915 a gentleman's morning coat suit, including waistcoat, would cost £4 10s.

George's son Don joined the business in 1923, and Ernest's son Ernest junior three years later, and both eventually became partners. The shop finally closed down in 1963, after which Don continued on his own in premises in Southampton Road for twelve years, before he eventually retired in 1975.

This photograph was taken in 1912, and shows the tailors' workroom at the rear of 9, St. Thomas' Street. The men are seen in the cross-legged position at which they sat throughout the working day, on two levels – the top board at the rear, and the lower board in the foreground. They used heavy irons to press the garments, up to 12 lbs. in weight, which were heated on a coke stove stoked up in the early morning. There were three Singer treadle sewing machines shared by the tailors.

Those seen in the picture are, left to right, back row: George Jenvey, his father and founder of the business John Jenvey, Charles Rogers, George Hallett, and Freddie Knight; front row: William Knight, Reginald Munden, George Kennedy, the other son of the founder Ernest Jenvey, and Mickey Rowe.

74 · Tow-Barges – Early Car Ferries

Cargo was shipped to the Isle of Wight from May, 1836, in specially designed tow-boats, resembling half-barges with a gate across the stern. They were hauled between Lymington and Yarmouth by the tug-boats *Carrier* and *Jumsey* during the winter months, and by the paddle-steamers in the summer. As can be seen from these photographs, the cars were reversed into the barges, and driven off forwards at their destination. In 1913 nearly 700 cars were carried on the Lymington–Yarmouth route in this manner. Cattle were also transported, leading to frantic scenes as stubborn animals refused to embark, some ending up in the water. Those arriving at Lymington were off-loaded by the railway station yard and then herded up Station Street, Gosport Street and the High Street to Mr. John Topp's 'knacker's' yard to the rear of his butcher's shop at 20, High Street; one of his specialities was pickled tongues. On one occasion the *Solent* paddle-steamer's excessive speed led to the tow-barge stern going down under the sea, so that it sank in deep water off Yarmouth with cars still on board.

Tow-barges continued to operate on this passage until the introduction of the revolutionary MV *Lymington*, which came into service on May 1st, 1948. Built on the Clyde, the double-ended vessel was the first British ferry to use Voith-Schneider propulsion, which enabled her to move in any direction without rudders. After early teething problems, she made seven round crossings daily, accommodating 400 passengers and 16 cars which drove directly on and off specially constructed slipways. In 1948 the vessel carried 4,000 cars, compared with less than 2,500 on passage the previous year. On March 4th, 1948, the larger MV *Farringford* (named after Lord Tennyson's house on the Isle of Wight) was added to the Lymington–Yarmouth route. Built in Dumbarton, she could carry 320 passengers and 32 cars – but owing to financial restraints after the Second World War, was a diesel-electric paddle vessel. By 1955, 42,000 cars made this crossing, and on September 21st, 1959, the Troon built MV *Freshwater* was added to the fleet. The River was dredged in

Loading cars at Lymington.

Unloading at Yarmouth.

1971 to permit two vessels to pass within its narrow confines. Three identical Voith-Schneider ships were ordered from Dundee – the *Cenwulf* which came on passage in October, 1973, to replace the *Lymington*; the *Cenred* in January, 1974, to replace the *Farringford*; and the *Caedmon*, which operated from Portsmouth until joining her sister ships at Lymington in November, 1983.

Index